NATIONAL GALLERY OF IRELAND

To Frank and Mary
with our love
Brendan, Johanna
Phelan Rossa
and Hannah
Christmas '94

Raymond Keaveney, Michael Wynne,
Adrian Le Harivel and Fionnuala Croke

National Gallery
of Ireland

SCALA BOOKS

© National Gallery of Ireland 1990

First published 1990
by Scala Publications Ltd
3 Greek Street
London W1V 6NX

ISBN 1 870248 59 7

Designed by Alan Bartram
Edited by Paul Holberton
Produced by Scala Publications
Filmset by August Filmsetting, St Helens, England
Printed and bound by Graphicom, Vicenza, Italy

FRONT COVER
Hugh Douglas Hamilton, *Frederick Hervey, Bishop of Derry and fourth Earl of Bristol, with his granddaughter Lady Caroline Crichton in the gardens of the Villa Borghese, Rome,* c.1788 (detail)

BACK COVER
Nicolas Poussin, *Acis and Galatea,* c.1629/31 (detail)

Contents

Introduction

The aspiration to establish a permanent collection of Old Master pictures in Ireland can be traced back at least to the second half of the eighteenth century. In 1766 the Society of Artists considered the establishment of a permanent gallery of pictures in its new premises in William Street, Dublin. A plan formally to establish a National Gallery was later instigated during the Viceroyalty of the Duke of Rutland, 1784-87. This initiative got as far as the appointment of a Keeper, the Flemish artist Peter de Gree, to oversee the formation of a collection, but the death of the Duke put an end to the project.

The organization of the Irish Industrial Exhibition of 1853 provided a new and effective stimulus to the long held wish for a permanent gallery. The exhibition project was supported by William Dargan who had amassed a considerable personal fortune pioneering the establishment of the Irish railway system. To commemorate in some substantial manner his extraordinary public-spiritedness in underwriting this great event, which had cost over £88,000, it was resolved to convene a public meeting in the Round Room of the Rotunda on 14 July 1853. Among the resolutions passed at this meeting was the following: 'That while we rejoice in being able to congratulate Mr Dargan . . . we are yet of the opinion that a great and combined exertion should be made throughout the country, to perpetuate, in connexion with his name, the rememberance of the good he has effected . . .'. No immediate decision was made as to the exact nature of this 'great and combined exertion' since its realisation was contingent on the extent of funding available.

After due deliberation it was eventually decided that a specially elected Testimonial Committee should cooperate with the newly established Irish Institution, a body formed in November 1853 'for the Promotion of Art in Ireland by the formation of a permanent Exhibition in Dublin, and eventually of a National Gallery'. Many of the members of the Irish Institution had assisted with the management of the Fine Arts Hall in the glazed pavilions of the Industrial Exhibition. The Testimonial Committee raised £5,000 towards the establishment of the Gallery and such was the success of their campaigning that within a year, in August 1854, an Act of Parliament was passed formally to establish the National Gallery of Ireland, and £6,000 of Government money was voted towards the funding of its construction. The total building cost of a gallery was at that time calculated at £11,000.

In many respects the foundation of a major public collection in the wake of a great industrial exhibition has close parallels with the founding of the Victoria and Albert Museum immediately following the Great Exhibition held at South Kensington in 1851. Indeed the Irish architect Francis Fowke, who had been entrusted with the design of the early buildings of the London institution, was given responsibility for the design of Dublin's new National Gallery. The brief for the Gallery, to be sited on the northern flank of Leinster Lawn, the site of the Industrial Exhibition of 1853, was to a very great extent influenced by the fact that the new building was to mirror as closely as possible, essentially in its exterior parts, Frederick Clarendon's design for the new Natural History Museum recently commissioned for the southern flank of Leinster Lawn. Fowke was called in to manage the design of the new gallery following dissatisfaction with earlier plans drawn up by the architect Charles Lanyon. Lanyon had been invited to submit alternative proposals to the plans presented by the artist George Mulvany, later to be appointed the Gallery's first Director in September 1862.

The foundation stone of Fowke's building was laid in January 1859 and construction took five years to complete. When opened to the public the new gallery, which had eventually cost more than £28,000 to erect, boasted some of the most advanced facilities of any museum of its time. These included sophisticated top-lit galleries for the display of the collection which, in evening time, was illuminated by over 2,000 gas burners. The threat of fire was diminished by the use of a special method of floor construction which involved combining iron girders and concrete casing, a forerunner of modern reinforced concrete. Even the acoustic quality of the Minton tiles used for the flooring was carefully considered. Virtually the last act in the long preparations for the Gallery's inauguration on 30 January 1864 was the positioning of the great bronze statue of William Dargan by Thomas Farrell on the Gallery forecourt in December of 1863.

When first opened to the public the collection consisted of just 125 paintings, including 28 loans, with the ground floor exhibition space given over to an arrangement of sculpture and plaster casts. The task of amassing a collection for a major public institution had not been easy as the Dublin Gallery did not incorporate, unlike many of its foreign counterparts, some great princely or private collection to form the basis of its holdings. In consequence, it was essential that, long before the inauguration of the building, a campaign be launched to acquire a suitable selection of paintings for display to the public.

Such a process was set in motion even before the formal establishment of the Gallery when the Irish Institution held its first exhibition in the rooms of the Royal Hibernian Academy in Lower Abbey Street on 2 January 1854. The Institution was empowered to accept in trust any paintings or financial donations destined for a future National Gallery. By 1855, eleven pictures had been secured for the collection. The following year marked an even more important advance when 16 paintings, many from the celebrated collection of Cardinal Fesch, were purchased in Rome for £1,700 through the agency of Robert Macpherson (1811-72). Later the same year a further 23 works were acquired from the persuasive Macpherson for a sum of £1,633. All 39 paintings were purchased on the evidence of pencil sketches, supplied by Macpherson, with funds generously lent by the Lord Chancellor, Maziere Brady, who at the time was a member of the Board of

Richard Thomas Moynan
Dublin 1856 – 1906 Dublin
Taking measurements: the artist copying a cast in the hall of the National Gallery of Ireland, 1887
Canvas, 99.5 × 62 cm
Purchased, 1989; NGI 4562

Governors and Guardians of the Gallery. Among the pictures acquired were large canvases by Giulio Cesare Procaccini [see p.23], Palma Giovane, Carlo Maratti [p.26] and two great compositions by Giovanni Lanfranco [p.26].

This bulk purchase of almost 40 pictures was to be unique in the process of building the collection. Once sufficient paintings had been acquired to cover the available exhibition space there was less pressure on the Board to consider acquiring works on such a scale. From 1864 onwards the growth of the collection progressed at a more measured pace. Also, there was a switch of emphasis from the pursuit of Italian masters to the acquisition of works from the Low Countries and from Spain and France. At the time of the opening of the Gallery Italian paintings had accounted for more than 50% of the works on view. The years leading up to the turn of the century were particularly remarkable for the growth of the collection of Dutch and Flemish paintings. For the most part, these were purchased individually or in small lots at auction in London, or occasionally on forays to the Continent.

Gradually the collection was beginning to assume the character of a broad, well balanced survey of European art with a degree of thoroughness which belied the institution's modest resources. From 1866 onwards an annual purchase grant was established at £1,000, that very modest sum being increased to £2,000 only in 1937. Given the lack of adequate funding the quality of the purchases made during the early years of the Gallery is very remarkable indeed. Among the most notable acquisitions made before the turn of the century were Rembrandt's *Rest on the Flight into Egypt*, which was obtained in 1883 for £514 [p.42]; *St Peter finding the Tribute Money* by Rubens in 1873 for £75 [p.56]; *The Immaculate Conception* by Zurbarán in 1886 for 42 guineas [p.66]; *The attempted martyrdom of Sts Cosmas and Damian* by Fra Angelico in 1886 for £73 10s [p.14]; *The Lamentation* by Poussin in 1882 for £503 [p.72].

By the year 1891, as a result of the purchasing policy adopted by the Board, the collection had grown to such an extent that the available accommodation was proving inadequate and serious consideration needed to be given to the problem of providing an extension to Fowke's building. In that year, the Director, Henry Doyle, reported to the Board that 'in the Great Gallery of Old Masters recourse has already been had to the system of erecting Screens in the centre of the floor for the exhibition of some of the smaller and more important pictures'. The desirability of constructing a new wing had become a necessity when the Dowager Countess of Milltown, in a letter written in October 1897 to the Director, Walter Armstrong, expressed the intention of presenting to the Gallery, in memory of her husband, 'the Pictures, Prints, works of Art and antique Furniture now at Russborough' (Russborough House was the country seat of the Earls of Milltown). The next extension was soon agreed and the design entrusted to Thomas Newenham Deane who had been in consultation with the Board about such a facility since

1891. Construction of the new wing began in late 1899 and it was inaugurated almost four years later, in March 1903. The Milltown gift, which included almost 200 pictures, a number of which had been collected on the Grand Tour, were displayed in the upper galleries of the new building. The paintings exhibited included works by Poussin, Panini [p.28], Dandini [p.28] and some family portraits by Pompeo Batoni [p.32].

Another notable endowment which occurred at this time was the bequest by Henry Vaughan of 31 watercolours by J M W Turner. This addition to the collection considerably enhanced the already burgeoning holding of prints and drawings which was advancing, *pari passu*, with the growth of the collection of oil paintings. Already, in 1864, Mulvany had purchased two small drawings by Federico Zuccari at the Watkins Brett sale at Christie's. In 1866 he attended the sale of Dr Wellesley's collection where he acquired a number of Renaissance drawings by Mantegna, Lorenzo di Credi, Antonio del Pollaiuolo and Parmigianino. In 1872 53 watercolours and drawings, including examples by Gainsborough, John Robert Cozens and Philippe Jacques de Loutherbourg, were presented by the noted English collector William Smith (1808-76) with a further 79 works entering the collection in 1876 under the terms of his will.

The National Gallery of Ireland, like most national institutions, suffered a reduction in financial support during the Great War, with its purchase fund abolished between the years 1914 and 1919. An even greater loss for the Gallery at this time was the death of Sir Hugh Lane (1875-1915), who drowned when the *Lusitania* went down off Cork in May 1915. Lane, perhaps the Gallery's most talented and certainly its most generous director, was a gifted connoisseur who had the remarkable talent of appreciating both modern and Old Master paintings as well as being keenly concerned about the development of the native Irish school of painting. After travelling the Continent as a young man, he moved to London where he learned the trade of picture dealing with Colnaghi's and the Marlborough Gallery, before setting himself up in business in 1898. In 1904 he was appointed a Governor and Guardian of the National Gallery of Ireland. At this time his principal ambition was the establishment of a Gallery of Modern Art in Dublin. He was to be sadly frustrated in this aspiration (and the unfortunate consequences of this failure are still to be felt today as some of his most treasured Impressionist pictures travel back and forth between Dublin and London, like lost souls). His interest in Old Master pictures brought him more satisfaction. In 1914 he was appointed Director of the Gallery and immediately proceeded to endow the institution with a series of generous gifts, beginning with El Greco's *St Francis* [p.61]. Even in death his munificence remained unabated and in his will he bequeathed the bulk of his estate to the Gallery, including a number of important paintings. Among the most notable were masterpieces by Sebastiano del Piombo [p.20], Claude [p.73], Poussin [p.72], van Dyck [p.58], Lawrence [p.97], Hogarth [pp.92–93] and Gainsborough [p.94].

His residuary estate continues to provide funds for the purchase of works of art for the collection.

Another outstanding Gallery benefactor was George Bernard Shaw (1856-1950), who bequeathed to it a third part of the royalties of his estate. The Gallery had obviously been an important element in the Dublin upbringing of the playwright who wrote of his experiences there: 'Let me add a word of gratitude to that cherished asylum of my boyhood, the National Gallery of Ireland. I believe I am the only Irishman who has ever been in it, except the officials. But I know that it did much more for me than the two confiscated medieval Cathedrals so magnificently "restored" out of the profits of the drink trade'. The Shaw fund, as it is now known, has served the Gallery magnificently since its resources were first applied to the purchase of Domenico Tintoretto's *Venice* in 1959. Other purchases through this fund have included *Abraham and the three angels* [p.62] by El Mudo; *Marie-Julie Bonaparte with her daughters* [p.79] by Gérard; *The funeral of Patroclus* [p.78] by Jacques-Louis David and, most recently, *Two women in a garden* by Emil Nolde [p.38].

With the continued growth of the collection, the need for a further extension again became an issue for discussion as early as the 1930s. In 1951 Thomas McGreevy, who was then Director, argued for the provision of additional accommodation. The campaign continued until 1962, when £277,000 was made available for a new wing. Designed by Frank du Berry of the Office of Public Works, this facility was opened to the public in September 1968, providing the Gallery not only with additional exhibition space but also a conservation studio, library, lecture theatre and restaurant. The rehang of the collection at this time proved a revelation as many of the great Baroque pictures, which had long gone out of fashion and had languished in storage for decades, could be displayed and admired.

In many respects the Gallery's holding of French paintings had grown more slowly than the other Continental schools. This pattern was to change rapidly in the 1960s. With the availability of additional exhibition space and access to funds from the Shaw bequest, Thomas McGreevy, and later James White, who was appointed Director in 1964, set about redressing the balance. Works by Courbet [p.80], David [p.78], Fragonard [p.76], Jacques Yverni [p.70] and Vouet [p.70] were purchased for the collection. The French school was further enhanced in 1978 when 93 paintings, presented to the Nation in 1950 by Sir Alfred Chester Beatty, were formally transferred to the Gallery. This collection was composed almost entirely of works by French artists, including Courbet, Millet [p.85], Couture [p.81], Meissonier [p.83] and Tissot [p.83], and artists such as Fromentin [p.82], Berchère and Gérôme [p.82] who reflected his interest in the Orient; this interest is even more substantially evidenced in the great library and museum which this modern Maecenas established in Dublin in 1953 to house one of the world's finest collections of Islamic, Mughal, Chinese and Japanese art.

Very recently the Gallery has been the fortunate recipient of two outstanding benefactions. In 1987 it received fourteen paintings and drawings from the estate of Máire MacNeill Sweeney. Included in the bequest, made in memory of her husband, John L Sweeney, were a *Still life with a mandolin* [p.68] by Picasso and a painting of *Pierrot* [p.68] by Gris. In the same year, incredibly, the Gallery received another extraordinary collection of pictures, seventeen masterpieces from Russborough House, today the home of Sir Alfred and Lady Beit. Their most generous gift includes some of the finest examples of Spanish, Dutch and British art, with stunning compositions by Velázquez [p.63], Murillo [pp.64–65], Jacob van Ruisdael [p.44], Jan Steen [p.49] and Gainsborough [p.94].

It is heartening to note in the light of these most magnificent donations that the courage, vision and generosity shown by those who were instrumental in the founding of the National Gallery, all those many years ago, continues to bear fruit and to inspire modern generations to emulate the vision of our ancestors, to whom we all owe a great debt of gratitude.

RAYMOND KEAVENEY
Director
National Gallery of Ireland

Italian School

The Gallery's earliest acquisitions of Italian art included a number of quality copies of acknowledged masterpieces, most notably two fine reproductions of Raphael's *Transfiguration* (acquired 1864) and *Santa Cecilia* (presented 1866). With regard to the acquisition of original works, many were initially appreciated more for their size than their pedigree, as they were needed to cover the vast hanging space of the great upper gallery. Large canvases by Giovanni Lanfranco, Giulio Cesare Procaccini, Pietro della Vecchia, Andrea Celesti, Palma Giovane, Carlo Maratta and Padovanino were among the paintings negotiated from Robert Macpherson in Rome, on the evidence of pencil sketches, in 1856. Such works would not have been considered exceptional at the time of purchase and it is only in recent times that their true merit has been more fully appreciated. Indeed, in the past, as the collection 'improved', many were despatched to storage for long periods. The two great Lanfranco compositions on the theme of the Eucharist [p.26], the Maratta *Europa and the Bull* [p.26] and Procaccini's *St Charles Borromeo in glory* [p.23] were so treated, though they are now acknowledged as outstanding examples of seventeenth-century Roman art. Forty years later, with the arrival of the Milltown gift (1902), the Gallery established an outstandingly representative collection of Florentine seventeenth-century art with paintings by Dandini, Lorenzo Lippi and Ficherelli [pp.27–28].

Other aspects of the Gallery's holdings of Italian art built up more slowly over the years. Many of the early 'Primitives' were acquired by Robert Langton Douglas whilst he was Director (1916-23). During his term of office he bought works by Silvestro dei Gherarducci (as Taddeo di Bartolo), Girolamo di Benvenuto, and Biagio d'Antonio (as Botticini). Later, in 1940, the Gallery purchased from him the rare school of Rimini *Noli me tangere* [p.13]. An early Renaissance masterpiece which came from the same source was Paolo Uccello's *Madonna and Child* [p.14], which entered the collection in 1909 as the work of Lorentino d'Arezzo. Fra Angelico's *Attempted martyrdom of Sts Cosmas and Damian* [p.14] was acquired earlier, at auction in London in 1886, while more recently Giovanni di Paolo's compelling, archaic *Crucifixion* [opposite] was added to the collection in 1964 by James White.

Amongst the earliest Renaissance pictures to grace the exhibition rooms was Marco Palmezzano's *St Philip Benizzi*, which was one of the works obtained from Robert Macpherson in Rome in 1856. In 1887 Luca Signorelli's predella panel, *Christ in the House of Simon the Pharisee*, from his altarpiece for Sant'Agostino in Siena, was acquired at auction in London for £178 10s. Other significant purchases were to be made in 1896 and 1931 when the classically inspired *Judith with the head of Holofernes* by Mantegna [p.16] and Perugino's languorous *Pietà* [p.17] entered the collection. Sebastiano del Piombo's portrait of Cardinal Antonio Ciocchi del Monte [p.20] formed part of the Lane bequest (1918).

Among the works purchased in Rome in 1856 were three sixteenth-century North Italian paintings: Jacopo Bassano's *Holy Family with donors*; Leandro Bassano's *Visit of the Queen of Sheba to Solomon* [p.21] and Palma Giovane's *Virgin and Child with saints and angels*. The charming Moroni portrait, *A widower with his two children* [p.19], was acquired by Mulvany in 1866. In 1882 Henry Doyle bid at the Hamilton Palace sale for a number of paintings, including the *Resurrection* by Antonio Palma, then considered to be by Bonifazio de' Pitati. Some three years later Doyle obtained Titian's *Ecce Homo* [p.20] at the Sir William Knighton sale at Christie's. The same artist's portrait of Baldassare Castiglione, which at one time belonged to Queen Christina of Sweden, formed part of the Lane bequest of 1918. Tintoretto's portrait of a Venetian senator [p.21] entered the collection in 1945.

Francesco Guardi's small, sparkling *Doge wedding the Adriatic* [p.30] was acquired in May 1864, just five months after the opening of the Gallery. Other eighteenth-century pictures to enter the collection before the turn of the century were two very fine Bellotto views of Dresden [p.30], which were secured for the Gallery at the M B Naryschkine sale in Paris in 1883 for £379, and Giovanni Battista Tiepolo's *Allegory of the Immaculate Conception* [p.31] acquired at auction in 1891 for 50 guineas. The Milltown gift of 1902 brought about the entry into the collection of a number of fine views of Rome by Panini [p.28] as well as some family portraits by Pompeo Batoni, including one of Joseph Leeson, first Earl of Milltown [p.32], the builder of Russborough House.

Giovanni di Paolo
Siena 1403? – 1483 Siena
The Crucifixion
Tempera on panel, 163 × 99 cm
(216 × 170 cm including restored
terminals)
Purchased, 1964 (Shaw fund); NGI 1768

11

1

Novgorod school
Early 15th century
St George and the Dragon
Tempera on panel, 73.5 × 63 cm
Purchased, 1968 (Shaw fund); NGI 1857
The icons in the Gallery's collection form
an introduction to the early Italian paintings which were influenced by the long
history of Byzantine art. The large size of
this magnificent example of the Novgorod
school, as well as its relatively late date,
may indicate that it was painted for a
church or chapel rather than a private
house. By the 15th century St George was
venerated in the districts of northern
Russia as the patron saint of agricultur-
alists and their herds. As one of the best
loved saints of these regions he was often
depicted slaying the dragon personifying
paganism and magical practices.

2

Constantinople school
***c.*1325 (margin 15th century)**
The Virgin and Child Hodigitria; (in the
margin) *St John the Baptist and twelve
Prophets*
Tempera on panel, 135 × 111 cm
Purchased, 1968 (Shaw fund); NGI 1858

1

2

3
Rimini school
14th century
The Crucifixion and Noli me tangere
Panel, 30 × 21 cm
Purchased, 1940; NGI 1022

4
Andrea di Bartolo
Active in Tuscany 1389 – 1428
St Galganus
Tempera on panel, 30 × 38 cm
Purchased, 1942; NGI 1089

3

4

1

2

1
Fra Angelico
Vicchio di Mugello 1387 –
1455 Rome
The attempted martyrdom of Sts Cosmas
and Damian with their brothers, 1438-40
Tempera on panel, 36 × 46 cm
Purchased, 1886; NGI 242
This brilliantly painted predella panel originally formed part of the great altarpiece
executed for the high altar of the church
attached to the Dominican convent of San
Marco in Florence. The work was commissioned by Cosimo de' Medici from Fra
Angelico to replace the earlier painting by
Lorenzo di Nicolò which, in 1438, Cosimo
had agreed to present to the convent of
San Domenico at Cortona. The altarpiece
was removed from the church in the 17th
century and today the main panel, which
shows the two saints kneeling, in the com-
pany of other saints, in the presence of the
Madonna and Child, is on view in the
Museo di San Marco in Florence. The dis-
membered predella panels which illustrate
the legend of the twin saints and their
three brothers, especially their martyrdom, are distributed among museums in
Munich, Paris and Washington.

2
Paolo Uccello
Pratovecchio Casentino 1397 –
1475 Florence
Virgin and Child, c.1440
Tempera on panel, 58 × 37 cm
Purchased, 1909; NGI 603
Uccello's fascination with mathematical
perspective is evident even in this small
panel: the Virgin and Child are placed before a niche which has a scalloped shell
design to convince us of its roundness,
and their haloes have been decorated with
a geometric design. The Child, leaping
playfully out of His mother's arms, steps
across a painted ledge, thereby appearing
to break down the division between
spectator and picture space.

3
Master of the Lucchese Immaculate
Conception
Active in Tuscany 15th century
Portrait of a musician
Panel, 51 × 36 cm
Purchased, 1897; NGI 470

4
Zanobi di Jacopo Machiavelli
Florence 1418 – 1479 Pisa?
The Virgin and Child enthroned with Sts
Bernardino of Siena, Mark, Louis of
Toulouse and Jerome
Panel, 133 × 150 cm
Purchased, 1861; NGI 108

3

4

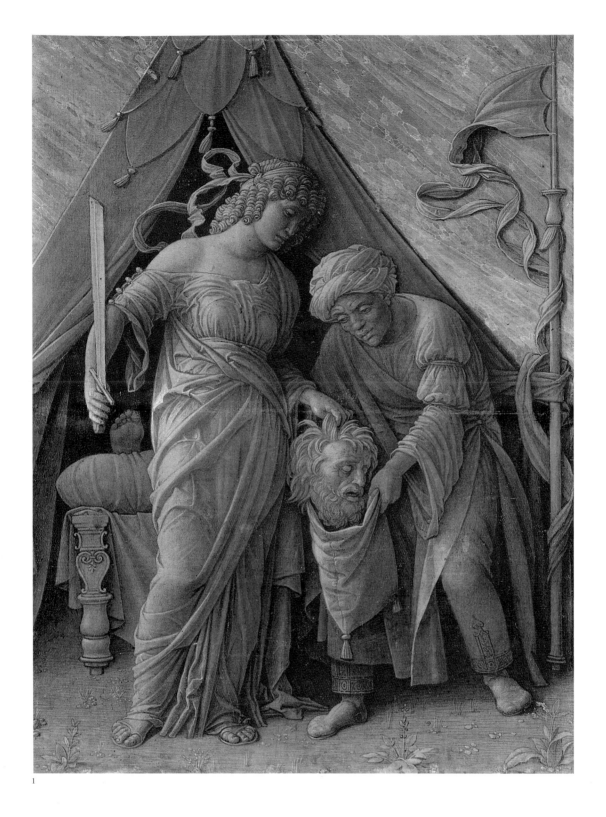

1

1

Andrea Mantegna
Isola di Carturo *c.*1431 – 1506 Padua
Judith with the head of Holofernes
Tempera on linen, 48.1 × 36.7 cm
Purchased, 1896; NGI 442
Mantegna was the Renaissance artist perhaps most fascinated by the heritage of
classical Rome. This composition has been
painted in *grisaille* in order to give the
impression that the image has been carved
in *pietra dura* in imitation of a Roman relief. The image of Judith beheading the As-
syrian chief (Judith 134, 9–10) had a
special significance for the small city states
of medieval and Renaissance Italy, as they
were under constant threat from their
more powerful neighbours.

2

Pietro Perugino
Città della Pieve *c.*1448 –
1523 Fontignano
*Pietà, c.*1500
Panel, 169.5 × 171.5 cm
Purchased, 1931 (Lane fund); NGI 942

3

Marco Palmezzano
Forlì 1458/63 – 1539 Forlì
The Virgin and Child enthroned, with Sts
John the Baptist and Lucy, 1513
Panel, 218 × 188 cm
Purchased, 1863; NGI 117

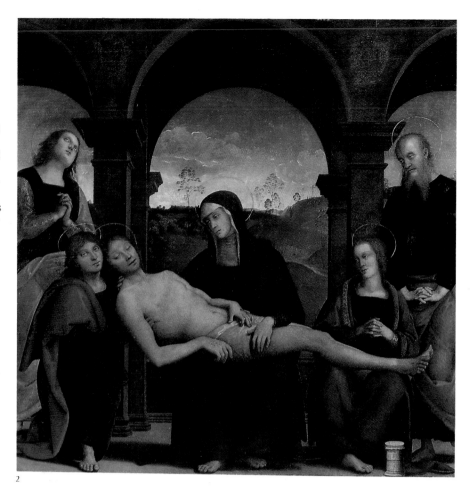

2

3

1

Francesco Francia
Bologna *c*.1450 – 1517/18 Bologna
Lucretia
Panel, 61 × 48 cm
Purchased, 1879; NGI 190

1

2

2
Lodovico Mazzolino
Ferrara *c.*1481 – 1530 **Milan**
Pharaoh and his host overwhelmed in the
Red Sea, 1521
Panel, 124 × 157 cm
Purchased, 1914; NGI 666
The date of this large panel is inscribed on
the base of the ritual vase beside the
figure of Aaron. Moses and the Israelites
are safely crowded on dry land while
Pharaoh and the Egyptian host struggle in
the water. Above, Jehovah and the archangel Michael admonish the drowning
soldiers. The extraordinary variety and vi-
vacity in the composition are emphasized
by Mazzolino's use of brilliant colours.
The town and seascape at the top of the
painting has a modern, almost surreal
quality, making this an exciting example
of Ferrarese mannerism.

3
Giovanni Cariani
Near Bergamo *c.*1485 – **after** 1547
Venice
The Virgin and Child with Sts John the
Baptist and Jerome
Canvas, 86 × 118 cm
Purchased, 1927; NGI 885

4
Giambattista Moroni
Bondio *c.*1520/25 – 1578 **Bergamo**
Portrait of a widower and his two children,
*c.*1565
Canvas, 126 × 98 cm
Purchased, 1866; NGI 105

3

4

1

1
Sebastiano del Piombo
Venice c.1485 – 1547 Rome
Cardinal Antonio Ciocchi del Monte
(1461-1533), c.1515
Canvas, 88 × 69 cm
Sir Hugh Lane bequest, 1918; NGI 783

2
Titian (Tiziano Vecellio)
Pieve di Cadore c.1480/5 –
1576 Venice
Ecce Homo, c.1558/60
Canvas, 73.4 × 56 cm
Purchased, 1885; NGI 75

3

3
Jacopo Tintoretto
Venice 1518 – 1594 Venice
Portrait of a Venetian senator, 1575/80
Canvas, 84 × 60 cm
Purchased, 1945; NGI 1122

4
Leandro Bassano
Bassano 1557 – 1622 Venice
The Visit of the Queen of Sheba to Solomon
Canvas, 168 × 112 cm
Purchased, 1856; NGI 97

4

1

1
Lavinia Fontana
Bologna 1552 – 1614 Rome
The Visit of the Queen of Sheba to Solomon,
*c.*1600
Canvas, 256.5 × 325 cm
Purchased, 1872; NGI 76
Lavinia Fontana was the first of Bologna's
numerous women painters to achieve re-
nown. This is one of her finest and most
ambitious paintings. The picture is, in all
probability, a portrait of the Duke of Mantua, Vincenzo I Gonzaga, with his wife
Leonora de' Medici. In 1600 they went to
Florence for the wedding of Marie de'
Medici and may have passed through Bologna on that occasion. The painting later
formed part of the collection of Prince
Napoleon in the Palais Royal in Paris, and
is one of the few pictures that were saved
from the fire there in 1872.

2
Giulio Cesare Procaccini
Bologna 1574 – 1625 Rome
St Charles Borromeo in glory with the
*Archangel Michael, c.*1620
Canvas, 385 × 252 cm
Purchased, 1856; NGI 1820
St Charles Borromeo (1538-84) was the
second son of Count Borromeo, the head
of a noble Lombard family. He was only
23 when he was made Cardinal Bishop of
Milan by his uncle Pius IV. A man of great
piety and asceticism, he sold all his pos-
sessions to assist with the relief of the
plague which devastated Milan in 1575. In
this painting by Procaccini he is being
taken up into Heaven in the presence of
the archangel Michael who is represented
weighing the soul of the saint. It is not
known who commissioned the work or
where it was originally intended to be displayed, though we know it was in the
church of San Carlo al Corso in Rome by
1628.

2

1

Orazio Gentileschi
Pisa 1563 – 1639 London
*David and Goliath, c.*1610
Canvas, 185.5 × 136 cm
Purchased, 1936 (Lane fund); NGI 980

2

Pensionante del Saraceni
Active Rome 1610 – 1620
St Peter denying Christ
Canvas, 104.4 × 133 cm
Purchased, 1948; NGI 1178

1

2

3
Mattia Preti
Taverna in Calabria 1613 –
1699 Valletta
The beheading of St John the Baptist, c.1650
Canvas, 135 × 97 cm
Purchased, 1864; NGI 366

4
Luca Giordano
Naples 1634 – 1705 Naples
St Sebastian tended by St Irene, 1650/5
Canvas, 152 × 127 cm
Presented by the third Duke of Leinster,
1868; NGI 79

3

4

1

2

Giovanni Lanfranco
Parma 1582 – 1647 Rome
The Multiplication of the Loaves and Fishes,
1620/5
Canvas, 229 × 426 cm
Purchased, 1856; NGI 72
This painting and its pendant, *The Last
Supper*, were commissioned for the Blessed Sacrament Chapel in the Basilica of San
Paolo fuori le Mura outside Rome. Lanfranco's decoration of the chapel consisted
of eight canvases, all of which treated the
theme of the Eucharist. The two National
Gallery paintings occupied the centre of
the side walls of the chapel. Clearly, from
the *sotto-in-su* perspective of the *Multiplication* they were intended to hang high,
probably over choir stalls. As with the
many other Baroque chapels which were
dedicated to the Blessed Sacrament this
commission was intended as a Counter-
Reformatory defence of the doctrine of the
Eucharist.

2

Carlo Maratta
Camerano 1625 – 1713 Rome
Europa and the Bull, 1680/5
Canvas, 248 × 424 cm
Purchased, 1856; NGI 81

3

Lorenzo Lippi
Florence 1606 – 1665 Florence
Medoro and Angelica, c.1630
Canvas, 173 × 238 cm
Milltown gift, 1902; NGI 1747

4

Felice Ficherelli
**San Gimignano c.1605 –
1669 Florence**
Lot and his Daughters, c.1650
Canvas, 159 × 176 cm
Milltown gift, 1902; NGI 1746

3

4

1

2

3

Cesare Dandini
Florence 1596 – 1656 Florence
Moses driving away the Shepherds,
1635/45
Canvas, 206 × 272 cm
Milltown gift, 1902; NGI 1683

2
Giovanni Paolo Panini
Piacenza *c.*1691 – *c.*1765 Rome
The Roman Forum, 1740
Canvas, 73 × 99 cm
Milltown gift, 1902; NGI 726

3
Giovanni Battista Passeri
Rome *c.*1610 – 1679 Rome
Party feasting in a garden
Canvas, 76 × 61.5 cm
Purchased, 1937; NGI 993
Passeri is better known as the biographer
of the lives of 17th-century artists in Rome
than as a painter, and this small canvas is
at present the only known signed work in
oils by Passeri. It serves as the basis for
the attribution of a small œuvre to the artist. The bright, eye-catching colours and
the festive setting belie the serious expres-
sions on the faces of the young people
who stare straight out at the spectator. The
full meaning of the subject is unclear despite the advance of a number of interpre-
tations. The feeling of clutter may explain
why, at some time, the statue on the left,
the antique urn and the Bacchic fountain
figure were overpainted. They were
revealed following restoration in 1983.

4
Giovanni Benedetto Castiglione
Genoa *c.*1610 – *c.*1655 Mantua
*The shepherdess Spako with the infant
Cyrus*, 1651/9
Canvas, 234 × 226.5 cm
Purchased, 1937 (Lane fund); NGI 994

5
Bernardo Strozzi
Genoa 1581 – 1644 Venice
Spring and Summer, *c.*1640
Canvas, 72 × 128 cm
Purchased, 1924; NGI 856

4

5

1

Bernardo Bellotto
Venice 1720 – 1780 Warsaw
Dresden from the right bank of the Elbe
above the Augustus Bridge, c.1750
Canvas, 51.5 × 84 cm
Purchased, 1883; NGI 181

2

Antonio Canaletto
Venice 1697 – 1768 Venice
St Mark's Square, Venice, with the Doge's
Palace, Campanile and Procuratorie Nuove,
1756?
Canvas, 46 × 77 cm
Purchased, 1885; NGI 286

3

Francesco Guardi
Venice 1712 – 1793 Venice
The Doge wedding the Adriatic, c.1780
Canvas, 39 × 57 cm
Purchased, 1864; NGI 92

2

3

4

5

4
Sebastiano Ricci
Cividale di Belluno 1659 –
1734 Venice
King Hieron II of Syracuse calls on
Archimedes to fortify the city, 1720s
Canvas, 104 × 84 cm
Purchased, 1942 (Lane fund); NGI 1099

5
Giovanni Antonio Pellegrini
Venice 1675 – 1741 Venice
Susanna and the Elders, c.1708/11
Canvas, 122.5 × 104 cm
Provenance uncertain, possibly from the
Harberton collection; NGI 1938

6
Giovanni Battista Tiepolo
Venice 1696 – 1770 Madrid
Allegory of the Immaculate Conception and
of Redemption, c.1760/70
Paper laid on canvas, 59 × 45 cm
Purchased, 1891; NGI 353

6

1

2

Pompeo Girolamo Batoni
Lucca 1708 – 1787 Rome
Joseph Leeson, afterward first Earl of
Milltown, 1744
Canvas, 137 × 102 cm
Milltown gift, 1902; NGI 701

Joseph Leeson (1711-83) was a member of a wealthy Dublin brewing family. In 1756 he was created Baron Russborough of Co. Wicklow and in 1763 he was elevated as Earl of Milltown, Co.Dublin. It was he who commissioned the construction of Russborough House in 1741 from Richard Castle. This portrait was painted on Leeson's first visit to Rome in 1744 and is the artist's earliest extant portrait of an English-speaking sitter. The portrait of Thomas Conolly (1738-1803) by Mengs is, like the Batoni, a work commissioned while on the Grand Tour (1758). Records

indicate that Conolly commissioned a second version of this work, one apparently intended for his home at Castletown House, Co.Kildare, and the other for his mother's house in Grosvenor Square in London. The bas-relief in the background is part of a frieze from a Roman sarcophagus which at that time was in the Capitoline Museum in Rome and which is now in the Louvre.

2
Anton Raphaël Mengs
Aussig 1728 – 1779 Rome
Thomas Conolly (1738-1803), 1758
Canvas, 135 × 98 cm
Purchased, 1983; NGI 4458

German and Early Netherlandish Schools

Although the German collection covers a wide chronology most works date from the fifteenth and sixteenth centuries. The core of the collection was acquired by the Gallery's first two Directors, George Mulvany and Henry Doyle, who bought a number of fine sixteenth-century portraits in London and Paris. These portraits, by Conrad Faber [p.36], Wolf Huber, Hans Suess von Kulmbach, Georg Pencz [p.36] and Bernhard Strigel [p.36], continue to be a highlight of the collection today. The development of the collection in the twentieth century is largely as a result of donations and purchases made in Dublin. Among the notable exceptions is the Styrian school *The Apostles taking leave of one another* [p.34]. This is a free-standing panel with *St Veronica's veil* on the reverse which was purchased by George Furlong in Vienna in 1936 along with the intricately crafted Salzburg school (*c*.1430) *Christ on the Cross with the Virgin Mary and John*.

A number of eighteenth- and nineteenth-century works were acquired by gift. Two imaginary interiors by Matthias Schiffer, dating to 1777 and presumably conceived as a pair, were part of the Milltown gift of 1902. Sir Alfred Chester Beatty's gift of 1950 included two paintings by Adolf Schreyer, *Arab horsemen* and *Eastern soldiers with a horse drinking*, both of which are typical of Schreyer's blend of realism and impressionistic colouring. More recently, in 1984, Director Homan Potterton purchased Emil Nolde's *Two women in a garden* in London, which at £356,000 is the second most expensive painting ever purchased for the Gallery [p.38].

One of the earliest Netherlandish acquisitions, by George Mulvany, was Gerard David's *Christ bidding farewell to His mother* [p.34], which has long been accepted as an important autograph work. Mulvany also purchased the *Two scenes from the life of a saint* by the Master of Sts Crispin and Crispinian, one of a series of which other panels have been identified in the Louvre and the Rijksmuseum, Amsterdam, and the painting of *St Luke painting the Virgin*, a copy of a detail from the well-known composition by Rogier van der Weyden (now in Boston). It bears the arms of Philippe de Bourgogne, with the heraldic achievement which Philippe was entitled to use between 1501 and 1517 when he was nominated as Bishop of Utrecht.

The majority of Early Netherlandish works were purchased in London and abroad. By happy coincidence Mulvany and Henry Doyle purchased the two portraits, of *Heinrich Knoblauch* and his sister *Katherina Knoblauch* [p.36], by Conrad Faber in two sales in Christie's, London, in 1885 and 1866 respectively.

A later acquisition of great importance was made by Robert Langton Douglas, Director from 1916 to 1923. In 1914 he purchased the right wing of a fifteenth-century triptych attributed to Marmion at the Earl of Ellenborough's sale, and later sold it to the Gallery. Max Friedlaender soon linked the painting to the central panel of an altarpiece now in the Metropolitan Museum, New York, and his attribution of the panels to the Master of St Augustine [p.35] has remained unchallenged.

A number of paintings were discovered in Irish collections. *The peasant wedding* by Pieter Brueghel the Younger [p.37], bought by Bodkin in 1928, was formerly in a private collection. A unique portrait group of *The Provost and Aldermen of the city of Paris*, dated 1568 and therefore the earliest such portrait in existence, was presented to the Gallery by the widow of the Hon Mr Justice James A. Murnaghan in 1974. Now catalogued as South Netherlandish school, the painting had been bought in Paris.

1

2

3

1
Styrian school
The Apostles taking leave of one another,
1494
Panel, 68.7 × 136 cm
Purchased, 1936; NGI 978

2
Gerard David
Oudewater before 1484 – 1523 Bruges
Christ bidding farewell to His mother,
*c.*1510
Panel, 119.6 × 61.4 cm
Purchased, 1869; NGI 13
This rare full-length *Christ*, inscribed *Fare-*
well my sweetest mother, I go now to be
offered for the salvation of mankind, shows
the moment that He leaves for Jerusalem
to begin the Passion story. The incident
was not described in the Gospels, but was
popularised as a theme for meditation in
the Middle Ages. David contrasts the con-
fident hand raised in blessing with a more
tentative gesture, and symbolically iso-
lates the statue-like figure in a bare 15th-
century room, lit evenly from an open
window. The panel was probably once the
left wing of a triptych, with the Virgin on
the right wing, but its history is unknown
before it was sold by the O'Shea family of
Co.Waterford. David's career declined in
the 1510s with the combined rivalry of
Antwerp painters and assistants like Ysenbrandt whose Dublin picture is a more pic-
turesque reworking of one by David.

3
Adriaan Ysenbrandt
Active in Bruges 1510 – 1551
Rest on the Flight into Egypt
Panel, 38.7 × 31.4 cm
Purchased, 1900; NGI 498

4
Master of St Augustine
Active probably in Ghent *c.*1490 –
1500
Scenes from the life of St Augustine
Panel, 136.1 × 66.4 cm
Purchased, 1919 (Lane fund); NGI 823

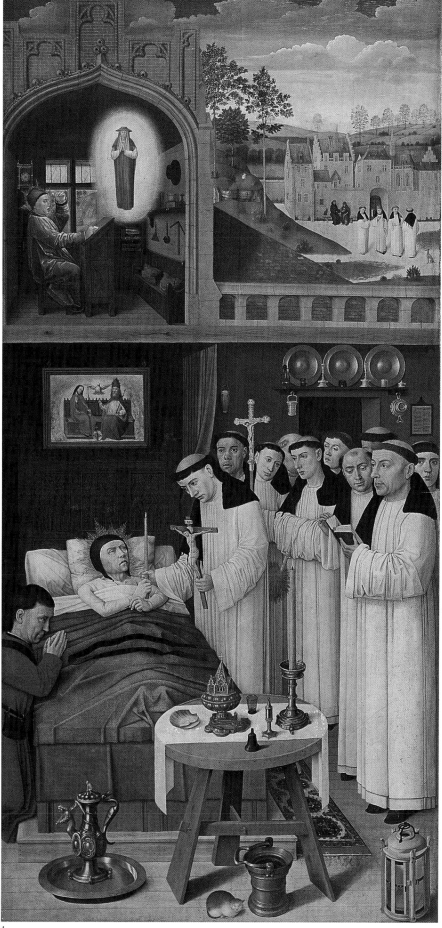

4

1
Bernhard Strigel
Memmingen 1460 – 1528 Memmingen
Johann II, Count of Montfort and Rothenfels
(died 1547), 1523
Panel, 30 × 22.5 cm
Purchased, 1866; NGI 6

2
Georg Pencz
Active in Nuremberg 1523 – 1550
Portrait of a man aged 28, 1549
Canvas, 84.1 × 64.5 cm
Purchased, 1864; NGI 1373

1

2

3

3
Conrad Faber
Creuznach before 1524 –
1552 Frankfurt
Katherina Knoblauch (1512/3-1542), 1532
Panel, 50.5 × 35.9 cm
Purchased, 1866; NGI 21

Katherina Knoblauch, like most of Faber's
sitters, belonged to the ruling house of
Limburg in Frankfurt-am-Main. She was 19
when Faber painted her and had been married for three years to Friedrich Rohrbach,
whose pendant portrait is now in the Art
Institute of Chicago. Her lavish outfit with
gilt thread and jewelled decoration, gold
belt, necklace and abundance of rings
indicates her wealth and status and is unusual for a German female portrait at this
date. The landscape, of river villages and
alpine mountains painted from a high
viewpoint, derives from a trip by Faber to
Passau, where he saw the work of Danube
school artists such as Huber. Faber was a
forgotten artist until this century and only
about forty portraits by him have been
identified. Many of them show a half-
length figure against a luminous distant
landscape, as here.

4
Marinus van Reymerswaele
Reymerswaele *c.*1495–
***c.*1567 Antwerp**
The Calling of St Matthew
Panel, 82.9 × 108.3 cm
Purchased, 1943 (part Lane fund); NGI 1115

5
Pieter Brueghel the Younger
Brussels *c.*1564 – *c.*1637 Antwerp
The peasant wedding, 1620
Panel, 81.5 × 105.2 cm
Purchased, 1928 (Lane fund); NGI 911

4

5

Emil Nolde
Nolde 1867 – 1953 Seebüll
Two women in a garden, 1915
Canvas, 73 × 88 cm
Purchased, 1984 (Shaw fund); NGI 4490
In the garden which surrounded his cottage on the island of Alsen, Nolde paints two women (his wife Ada on the right) who meet amongst a profusion of glowing flowers. This year was the most productive of his career, but the strong contrasts of colour and brooding sky reflect an inner melancholy, due both to political events and his intense response to nature. He wrote of flowers that they grow, give pleasure, then fade and are discarded, and he created a garden at each of his retreats in northern Germany. After early success with bright gardens, following his series of the *Life of Christ*, his subject matter became increasingly metaphoric, the Expressionist style fusing the work of modern artists he had seen with Old Master colourists such as Rubens and Titian. Nolde was called degenerate by the Nazis in the 1930s and forbidden to paint during the War years.

Dutch School

The Dutch School is one of the strongest in the entire collection. The Gallery holds a number of paintings of the highest order, among them Rembrandt's *Landscape with the Rest on the Flight into Egypt* [p.42], Jan Steen's *Village school* [p.48], Bol's *David's dying charge to Solomon* [p.43], Hobbema's *Wooded landscape – the path on the dyke* [p.45] and Jacob van Ruisdael's *Castle of Bentheim* [p.44].

Yet connoisseurs of Dutch painting look to Dublin not only for its holding of major masterpieces, but also for its broad range of excellent works by lesser artists. The large collection was assiduously formed in particular by the second Director, Henry Doyle, who held office from 1869 until 1892. Most of his purchases were made at Christie's in London. Doyle had a purchase grant of a mere £1,000 per annum, for all schools. While he paid £790 for a fine Jan Both *Italianate landscape* in 1880, he acquired the charming Moreelse portrait of a child for five guineas in 1885. A small landscape by Jacob van Ruisdael cost 420 guineas in 1873, while the extensive *Raid on a village* by Bleker was acquired for a mere fifteen guineas in 1885. In 1883 Doyle bid successfully for the beautiful, small Rembrandt *Landscape with the Rest on the Flight into Egypt* which he secured for the Gallery for £514.

Sir Henry Page Turner Barron Bt clearly had a very discriminating eye. This little known Irishman spent several decades as British Minister to the Court of Wurttemberg. Following his death, the Gallery received, in 1902, some excellent paintings including a number from the Dutch School. The Salomon van Ruysdael painting of *The halt* [p.45] is an excellent example of this artist's work. A banquet-piece by Willem Claesz. Heda strengthened the holding of Dutch still-life paintings. The untimely death of Sir Hugh Lane in the *Lusitania* tragedy of 1915 brought a splendid injection of Old Master paintings to the Gallery. Among these were Jan van Goyen's monochromatic *View of Rhenen-on-the-Rhine* [p.44], and a superbly painted portrait of a lady holding a glove [p.41], currently catalogued as studio of Rembrandt. The style in which the rich clothing is painted must surely lead eventually to the author's identification. In 1923 Robert Langton Douglas presented the Gallery with a *Brazilian landscape* by Frans Post [p.47], a type of view now widely sought. The gift of seventeen paintings by Sir Alfred and Lady Beit in 1987 further strengthened the Dutch Collection. Jan Steen's finely painted *Marriage Feast at Cana* [p.49] is surely one of that painter's most accomplished works, while Frans Hals's *Lute-player* [p.40] is a most striking picture, in a mode highly cultivated by Dutch artists of the period.

The foregoing paragraphs all concern the Golden Age of Dutch painting, namely the seventeenth century. The Gallery also has a small but significant number of Dutch eighteenth-century pictures. Johannes Petrus Horstok's portrait shows the sitter, *Jean-Jacques Dessont*, in a room with a number of pieces of eighteenth-century furniture. *A garland of flowers hanging from a bough*, with only a qualified attribution to Jacob Xavery is, nonetheless, a decorative picture of the highest quality. Johannes Hubert Prins's *The weigh-house on the Buttermarket, Amsterdam* is a very accurate rendition of an eighteenth-century streetscape as is Jan ten Compe's *Village with a windmill*. Cornelis Troost's depiction of two gentlemen in a lovely interior [p.53] is perhaps the artist's masterpiece.

1

2

3

40

1
Willem Duyster
Amsterdam 1599 – 1635 Amsterdam
Interior with soldiers, 1632
Panel, diameter 48.2 cm
Purchased, 1895; NGI 436

2
Frans Hals
Antwerp *c.*1580/3 – 1666 Haarlem
The lute player, *c.*1630
Canvas, 83 × 75 cm
Gift of Sir Alfred Beit Bt, 1987; NGI 4532
(Beit collection)
Hals's portraits are remarkable for their
sense of immediacy and spontaneity. The
pose of the lute player, turning three-
quarters towards the spectator and leaning
back slightly from the foreground area of
the canvas, contributes to this effect, as do
the quick, broad brushstrokes.

3
Dirck van Delen and Dirck Hals
Heusden 1605 – 1671 Arnemuiden;
Haarlem 1591 – 1656 Haarlem
An interior with ladies and cavaliers, 1629
Panel, 73 × 96.5 cm
Purchased, 1889; NGI 119

4
Studio of **Rembrandt**
Leyden 1606 – 1669 Amsterdam
Portrait of a lady holding a glove, 1632/33
Canvas, 72 × 62 cm
Sir Hugh Lane bequest, 1918; NGI 808

5
Willem Drost
Active 1652 – 1680
*Bust of a man wearing a large-brimmed
hat*, *c.*1654
Canvas, 64 × 55.7 cm
Purchased, 1889; NGI 107

4

5

1

1
Rembrandt van Rijn
Leyden 1606 – 1669 Amsterdam
Landscape with the Rest on the Flight into
Egypt, 1647
Panel, 34 × 48 cm
Purchased, 1883; NGI 215
The highlight of the Dutch collection is
surely this small panel depicting the *Rest*
on the Flight into Egypt. Horace Walpole in
1762 referred to it as a nightpiece, and the
composition is derived from Elsheimer's
Rest on the Flight painted in 1609, which
also shows the Flight taking place at night.
Rembrandt's dramatic use of chiaroscuro
heightens the atmospheric effect: the central figures are contained in the ovoid of
warmth and light created by the bonfire
which is tended by the little herdsboy,
while the moonlight draws attention to the
Italianate detail of the Claudean building
on the hilltop.

2

2
Pieter Lastman
Amsterdam? 1583? – 1633 Amsterdam
Joseph selling corn in Egypt, 1612
Panel, 57.6 × 88.2 cm
Purchased, 1927; NGI 890

3

4

5

3
Gerbrandt van den Eeckhout
Amsterdam 1621 – 1674 Amsterdam
Christ in the synagogue at Nazareth, 1658
Canvas, 61 × 79 cm
Purchased, 1885; NGI 253

4
Ferdinand Bol
Dordrecht 1616 – 1680 Amsterdam
David's dying charge to Solomon, 1643
Canvas, 171 × 230 cm
Deposited with the Irish Institution for the
National Gallery of Ireland by the Lord
Lieutenant, the Earl of St Germans, 1854;
NGI 47

5
Govert Flinck
Kleve 1615 – 1660 Amsterdam
Bathsheba's Appeal, 1651
Canvas, 105.5 × 152.6 cm
Purchased, 1867; NGI 64

1

1

Jacob Isaacksz. van Ruisdael
Haarlem *c.*1628/9
– 1682 Amsterdam
The Castle of Bentheim, 1653
Canvas, 110.5 × 144 cm
Gift of Sir Alfred Beit Bt, 1987; NGI 4531
(Beit collection)
Perhaps the finest Dutch landscape painter
of the 17th century, Ruisdael was probably
first taught by his father though he may
also have been apprenticed to his uncle
Salomon van Ruysdael (see *The halt*,
opposite). This dramatic view of Bentheim
castle is a relatively early work, painted
when Ruisdael was about 24 years old, yet
it has always been regarded as one of his
greatest masterpieces. Ruisdael has
dramatized the view by placing the castle
on a prominence with the village of
Bentheim nestling on the hillside.

2

Hendrick Avercamp
Amsterdam 1585/6 – 1634 Kampen
Scene on the ice, 1620
Panel, 20.5 × 43.8 cm
T Humphry Ward gift, 1900; NGI 496

2

3

44

3
Jan van Goyen
Leyden 1596 – 1656 The Hague
A view of Rhenen-on-the-Rhine, 1644
Panel, 64 × 94 cm
Sir Hugh Lane bequest, 1918; NGI 807

4
Salomon van Ruysdael
Naarden *c.*1600 – 1670 Haarlem
The halt, 1647
Canvas, 99 × 153 cm
Sir Henry Page Turner Barron bequest,
1901; NGI 507

5
Meindert Hobbema
Amsterdam 1638 – 1709 Amsterdam
A wooded landscape – the path on the dyke,
1663
Canvas, 105.5 × 128 cm
Gift of Sir Alfred Beit Bt, 1987; NGI 4533
(Beit collection)

4

5

1

2

3

1

Jan van Kessel
Amsterdam 1641/2 – 1680 Amsterdam
The Dam at Amsterdam, 1669
Canvas, 68 × 83.1 cm
Purchased, 1930; NGI 933

2

Jan Wijnants
Haarlem active 1643 – 1684 Amsterdam
The dunes near Haarlem, 1667
Canvas, 21.4 × 26 cm
Purchased, 1885; NGI 280

3

Anthonie de Lorme
Tournai *c.*1610 – 1673 Rotterdam
Interior of the St Laurenskerk, Rotterdam,
*c.*1660/5
Canvas, 87.1 × 73.7 cm
Purchased, 1903; NGI 558

4

Frans Post
Haarlem 1612 – 1680 Haarlem
A Brazilian landscape, 1660/5
Panel, 48.3 × 62.2 cm
Robert Langton Douglas gift, 1923; NGI 847
Post spent the years from 1636 until 1644
in Brazil as a member of the entourage of
the Governor-General Count Johan Mau-
rits van Nassau-Siegen. Back in Haarlem,
he continued to paint only Brazilian
scenes which are characterized by his use
of vivid blues and greens and exotic plant
and animal life. This imaginary landscape
dotted with sugar plantations was probably painted about twenty years after his
return to Holland.

5

Ludolf Bakhuisen
Emden 1631 – 1708 Amsterdam
The Arrival of the Kattendijk *at the Texel,*
22nd July 1702, 1702
Canvas, 133 × 111 cm
Purchased, 1883; NGI 173

4

5

47

1

1

Jan Steen
Leyden 1625/6 – 1679 Leyden
The village school, c.1665
Canvas, 110.5 × 80.2 cm
Purchased, 1879; NGI 226

Steen was an extremely productive painter,
and this is one of a number of schoolroom
scenes painted by him. In it he used his
three children, Catherina, Cornelis and Johannes, as models for the little girl, the
boy being punished and the boy holding a
paper. The punishment was not excessive
by 17th-century standards. Despite an
edict of 1655 which required that a school-
master be literate, there were still many
complaints made of school teachers in
17th-century Holland. Drinking was a
major problem and the bottles in the niche
probably allude to this.

2

Ascanius (Domenicus van Wijnen)
Amsterdam 1661 – *c*.1700
The Temptation of St Anthony
Canvas, 72 × 72 cm
Arthur Kay gift, 1901; NGI 527

3

Jan Steen
Leyden 1625/6 – 1679 Leyden
The Marriage Feast at Cana, 1665/70
Panel, 63.5 × 82.5 cm
Gift of Sir Alfred Beit Bt, 1987; NGI 4534
(Beit collection)

2

3

1

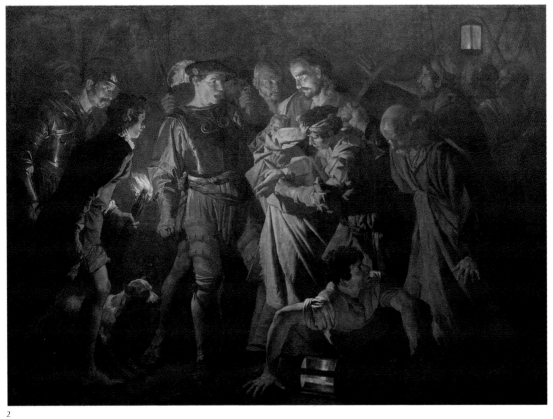

2

1
Gerrit van Honthorst
Utrecht 1590 – 1656 Utrecht
A feasting scene (the interior of a brothel),
1628
Canvas, 146 × 205 cm
Purchased, 1958; NGI 1379

2
Matthias Stomer
Amersfoort? *c*.1600 – *c*.1650 Sicily?
*The Arrest of Christ, c.*1641
Canvas, 201 × 279 cm
Sir George Donaldson gift, 1894; NGI 425

3
Karel Dujardin
Amsterdam? *c*.1622 – 1678 Venice
The riding school, 1678
Canvas, 60.2 × 73.5 cm
Purchased, 1903; NGI 544

4
Jan Baptist Weenix
**Amsterdam 1621 – *c*.1660-61 Huis ter
Mey near Utrecht**
*The sleeping shepherdess, c.*1658
Canvas, 72.5 × 61.1 cm
Sir Henry Page Turner Barron bequest,
1901; NGI 511

3

4

1

Willem Claesz. Heda
1593/4 – 1680/2 Haarlem
A banquet-piece, c.1635
Panel, 55.3 × 73.8 cm
Sir Henry Page Turner Barron bequest,
1901; NGI 514

2

Jan Davidsz. de Heem
Utrecht 1606 – Antwerp 1683
A vanitas fruit-piece, 1653
Canvas, 85.5 × 65 cm
Purchased, 1863; NGI 11

2

3
Godfried Schalcken
Made 1634 – 1706 The Hague
Pretiose recognised, 1655/70
Panel, 44.2 × 31.2 cm
Purchased, 1898; NGI 476
Schalcken's extraordinary attention to detail and the beautiful finish which he gives
to his works mark him out as belonging to
the *fijnshilderij* tradition in Dutch art, a
tradition which was centred in Leyden
where this delicate approach to painting
was made popular by Gerard Dou
(1613-75). This small, meticulously painted
panel illustrates an episode from Cer-
vantes's novella *La Gitanilla* (The Little
Gypsy). The subject was ideal for an artist
of Schalcken's skill as its interpretation is
dependant on the recognition of the tiny
mole on the breast of the heroine.

Constance, the daughter of noble
parents, had been stolen as an infant by
the gypsy woman Majombe who gave her
the name Pretiose. Don Juan falls in love
with her and she demands of him that he
live with her for two years among the gyp-
sies. During this period he is falsely ac-
cused of theft and kills one of those
arresting him. Pretiose begs the magistrate's wife to intercede for him
with her husband. It is at this point that
Majombe intervenes and declares that Pretiose is none other than the magistrate's
own daughter, an identification confirmed
by the mother who recognizes the mole
on the young woman's breast.

3

4
Cornelis Troost
Amsterdam 1696 – 1750 Amsterdam
*Jeronimus Tonneman and his son Jeronimus
('The Dilettanti)*, 1736
Panel, 68 × 58 cm
Purchased, 1909; NGI 497
Troost was the most talented of the Dutch
18th-century portraitists. Like Hogarth he
painted genre scenes of contemporary life
with a strong element of social satire. In
this double portrait, the elder Tonneman
clearly wanted to be portrayed as a connoisseur and patron of the arts and the
plaster reliefs and statue which decorate
the idealised interior were surely selected
as a warning against the vanity of such a
role. The young Tonneman plays an ele-
gant flute while the stucco roundel shows
Mercury killing Argus which he did after
lulling him to sleep with music. The other
relief shows *Time unveiling Truth*, by a
curious irony the younger Tonneman
stabbed his mistress the following year
and fled Holland on a voyage to the East
Indies.

4

Later Flemish School

There are today 81 Flemish paintings in the Gallery dating from the seventeenth to the nineteenth century, but the focus by early directors George Mulvany and Henry Doyle on Rubens and his circle has meant that over a third are by or after Rubens, Jordaens, van Dyck and David Teniers II. Even at the opening of the Gallery, animal and genre subjects by Pieter Boel and David Ryckart III took second place to *The Veneration of the Eucharist* [opposite] by Jordaens, probably thought a suitably fervent altarpiece to accompany the Italian Baroque paintings. It was acquired at the John Allnut sale for the modest sum of £84 when the artist was less valued than today. Its presence no doubt encouraged the Italo-Irish entrepreneur, Charles Bianconi, who established road-cars across Ireland for passengers and freight, to donate the other major Jordaens [p.56], formerly in Lord Northwick's collection. The finest Rubens, *St Peter finding the Tribute Money* [p.56], was once bought for the King of Poland. *The Annunciation*, which cost £720 in 1871, is now thought to be painted mainly by workshop assistants, though it once belonged to Prince Friedrich Hendrik of Orange and hung as an overmantel at Huis ten Bosch. The Barron bequest of Dutch and Flemish paintings in 1901 included the very detailed *Christ in the House of Martha and Mary* [p.57], a collaboration between Rubens (the figures) and Jan Brueghel II, son of the better known Jan 'Velvet' Brueghel and grandson of Pieter Breugel the Elder. The subject is given a novel exterior setting crowded with animals and flowers (many symbolic) and a backdrop of the Château de Mariemont, summer residence of the Spanish Regents in Flanders. Lucas van Uden also worked with Rubens; in his landscape titled *Peasants merrymaking* [p.59], David Teniers II painted the bucolic peasants. There are also five miniature copies by Teniers of Italian paintings in Archduke Leopold Wilhelm's collection in Brussels, which were in turn copied by engravers for the 1665 *Theatrum Pictorium*.

The Sir Hugh Lane bequest in 1918 included the stately van Dyck portrait of a boy, so evocative of wealth and culture in seventeenth-century Genoa [p.58]. Doyle had earlier purchased a van Dyck study of a *Naked youth*, related to his series of St Sebastian pictures, and the portrait of Frederick de Marselaer, a civic administrator in Brussels. The Snyders painting [p.57], also bequeathed by Lane, would seem to be a reminder of extravagant living without the moral overtones of Dutch artists like de Heem. The minutely detailed surface includes a squirrel, parrot and monkey, set amongst glass, metalwork and a collection of the exotic fruit for which Antwerp was renowned. The Lane fund allowed the purchase of a Siberechts [p.59] in superb condition. The theme of a farm cart at a ford is typical of his work before he went to England at the invitation of the Duke of Buckingham and painted mainly aerial views of country houses. There are variations of the theme in London, Antwerp and Lille, but the colours of *The farm cart* are particularly well preserved, with a high degree of finish in the trees and figures.

Jacob Jordaens
Antwerp 1593 – 1678 Antwerp
*The Veneration of the Eucharist, c.*1630
Canvas, 285 × 235.1 cm
Purchased, 1836; NGI 46
This overwhelming allegory of a central tenet of Roman Catholicism is today difficult to interpret fully, as it is not known for which church or religious Order it was painted. A woman on a lion holding the Eucharistic wafer in a monstrance is set above the rock of the Church. Sts Peter, Paul (left), Catherine, Rosalie and Sebastian (right) flank her and like the Latin Doctors of the Church below (Sts Augustine, Jerome, Gregory and Ambrose) are identified by their symbols and dress. The Christ Child, holding a flaming heart, triumphs over death and the Devil.

Jacob Jordaens
Antwerp 1593 – 1678 Antwerp
The Supper at Emmaus, c.1645/65
Canvas, 198.5 × 211.5 cm
Charles Bianconi gift, 1865; NGI 57

Peter Paul Rubens
Siegen 1577 – 1640 Antwerp
St Peter finding the Tribute Money, c.1618
Canvas, 199.4 × 218.8 cm
Purchased, 1873; NGI 38

In St Matthew's Gospel (17: 24–27) Christ tells Peter he will find money needed for taxes in the jaws of a fish. The scene is related here as the disciples and a passing woman respond in amazement to his discovery. This is an unusual subject in Flemish painting, and the two surviving depictions before Rubens were both commissioned appropriately for the chapels of fishermen's guilds. While Rubens worked on another version for the guild in Mechelen, he exchanged this picture, with eleven others, for antiquities belonging to Sir Dudley Carleton, English Ambassador at The Hague and noted connoisseur. In a celebrated incident, some pictures were returned as they were thought to be from the workshop, so Rubens wrote that he himself had painted the *St Peter*. Its authenticity has also been doubted at times since 1801, but the strongly lit, muscular figures and distinctive use of colour reveal the hand of Rubens.

1

2

3
Jan Brueghel II and Peter Paul Rubens
Antwerp 1601 – 1678 Antwerp;
Siegen 1577 – 1640 Antwerp
Christ in the house of Martha and Mary,
1628?
Panel, 64 × 61.9 cm
Sir Henry Page Turner Barron bequest,
1901; NGI 513

4
Frans Snyders
Antwerp 1579 – 1657 Antwerp
A banquet-piece, late 1620s
Canvas, 92.3 × 158 cm
Sir Hugh Lane bequest, 1918; NGI 811

3

4

1

2

Anthony van Dyck
Antwerp 1599 – 1641 London
A boy standing on a terrace, c.1625
Canvas, 188.3 × 125.3 cm
Sir Hugh Lane bequest, 1918; NGI 809
The boy may never be identified as the
history of the picture before it was bequeathed is unknown. It is one of nine
portraits of individual children painted for
rich Genoese families from 1621 to 1627,
when van Dyck made three long visits to
the city. These were exceptional commis-
sions at a time when children were generally painted in a minor role with their
parents. Although a child, the sitter has an
adult ease of command as he poses against
a background of draped column, balus-
trade and landscape view. Van Dyck's skill
is to suggest that these devices are as
natural and spontaneous as the dog which
jumps at his hand. The contrast of sombre
architecture and finely painted suit of
Genoese velvet gives a sense of bulk to the
sitter, who appears less introverted than
others van Dyck portrayed, who are generally dressed in black.

2
Lucas van Uden and David Teniers II
Antwerp 1595 – 1672 Antwerp;
Antwerp 1610 – 1690 Brussels
Peasants merrymaking, early 1640s
Canvas, 122.2 × 218 cm
Purchased, 1874, NGI 41

3
Jan Siberechts
Antwerp 1627 – *c.*1700 London
The farm cart, 1671
Canvas, 72.4 × 85.5 cm
Purchased, 1928 (Lane fund); NGI 900

3

59

Spanish School

Considering their small numbers, the Gallery's holding of Spanish paintings is remarkable both for its range and its quality. That Spanish art was, from the very start, considered to be important for the development of the collection is clear from the purchase of *The liberation of St Peter* by José Antolinez in 1859 and the subsequent spate of purchases immediately following the opening of the Gallery. It must be remembered, though, that works of the great Spanish masters were rarer than their Italian or Dutch counterparts and generally beyond the modest means of the Board. Despite these difficulties the patient and astute purchases of the various Directors have, over the years, gradually established a fascinating collection of some 50 works.

In the very early years of the Gallery, under Mulvany's direction, a number of fine works were added to the Antolinez, including Zurbarán's *St Diego of Alcala*, acquired in 1864 for just £5, and Murillo's portrait of *Josua van Belle*, which cost £100 in 1866 when acquired in London. Also purchased by Mulvany, in Madrid in 1865, was a *St Teresa of Avila* which has only recently been attributed to Juan Antonio de Frias y Escalante. Henry Doyle, Director from 1869 to 1892, continued the policy of opportunistic purchasing of Spanish art, his first acquisition being Murillo's *Infant John playing with a lamb* which he acquired in Paris in 1869 for £400, a considerable expenditure in those days for the Dublin gallery. Later, in 1886, he bid at auction for a painting representing *The Immaculate Conception*, then attributed to Valdés Leal [p.66]. Acquired for just 42 guineas, the work carried its old attribution until 1922 when it was recognized as a late work of Zurbarán. The attribution to Zurbarán was confirmed in 1981 when traces of the artist's signature were revealed during the course of cleaning. Other purchases by Doyle were a *St Jerome in the wilderness* by Luis Morales, acquired in 1872 for just £12, and a *St Onophrius* by Ribera acquired in 1879 for £50.

Walter Armstrong, who succeeded Doyle in 1892 and continued as Director until 1914, was also conscious of the merits of the Spanish School and travelled to Spain in 1905 to admire the great masters at first hand. In 1869 he had in fact published a book on Velázquez. But it was Goya who was to be the prime object of his attentions when pursuing acquisitions for the collection, and he purchased two works by the master within the space of just three years. In 1905 he bought the artist's *Lady in a black mantilla* in Paris for £600 and in 1908 the portrait of the Conde del Tajo for £975 [p.67]. Sir Hugh Lane (Direc-

tor 1914-15) also had a fascination for Goya, but he was to be less fortunate in his pursuit of works by the master. In 1914 he had to pay the considerable sum of £5,680 for a *Woman in a black shawl* at the Rouart sale in Paris in 1912. This work, which entered the collection in 1918 as part of his bequest, has recently been catalogued as 'follower of Goya' as it has proved difficult to establish Goya's authorship beyond dispute. Among the other paintings which Lane bequeathed to the Gallery were *St Francis receiving the stigmata* [opposite] by El Greco, *Jael and Sisera* by Pedro Núñez del Valle, and *The Virgin of the Rosary* by Sebastian de Llanos y Valdés.

Thomas Bodkin (Director 1927-35) obtained a third Zurbarán for the collection in London in 1933 when he purchased *St Rufina* [p.66] for 720 guineas. This painting had at one time formed part of the collection of King Louis-Philippe (a collection which had been assembled by Baron Isidore Taylor, whose father was Irish). In 1939, Bodkin's successor, George Furlong (Director 1935-50) acquired the fifteenth-century panel of *St Jerome translating the Bible* [opposite], employing the services of Langton Douglas who advised him that it would make a fine addition to the Gallery's collection of French paintings. It was only in 1941 that R C Post identified the painting as being by Nicolás Francés.

Thomas McGreevy (Director 1950-63), who had the great good fortune to have available monies from the Shaw fund to assist with the purchase of paintings, acquired two works by Murillo in April 1962, *The Holy Family* and *The penitent Magdalen*. In the same year he acquired the large canvas *Abraham and the three angels* by El Mudo [p.62], which had been commissioned by Philip II of Spain in 1575 for the guest rooms of the monastery of the Escorial. Another purchase made through the Shaw fund was Goya's *El sueño* [p.67], which was acquired by James White (Director 1964-80) in 1969.

Homan Potterton (Director 1980-88), though he never purchased any Spanish pictures, witnessed the greatest enrichment of this aspect of the collection to date when, in 1987, he received two extraordinary endowments. The Máire McNeill Sweeney bequest included two superb modern works, Picasso's *Still life with mandolin* and *Pierrot* by Gris. Even more extraordinary was the spectacular gift of seventeen pictures by Sir Alfred and Lady Beit which included eight Spanish masters, most notably the early *bodegón* by Velázquez, *The kitchen maid with the Supper at Emmaus* [p.63] and Murillo's complete set of six paintings on the theme of the Prodigal Son [pp.64-65].

1
Nicolás Francés
Burgundy? *c.*1400 – 1468 **Leon**
*St Jerome translating the Bible, c.*1430
Panel, 134.5 × 85 cm
Purchased, 1939 (part Lane fund); NGI 1013

2
El Greco (Domenikos
Theotokopoulos)
Crete 1541 – 1614 Toledo
St Francis receiving the stigmata, 1590/5
Canvas, 114.8 × 106.3 cm
Sir Hugh Lane gift, 1914; NGI 658

1

2

1

1

Juan Fernández de Navarrete 'El Mudo'
Logrono 1538? – 1579 Toledo
Abraham and the three angels, 1576
Canvas, 286 × 238 cm
Purchased, 1962 (Shaw fund); NGI 1721
The aged Abraham was visited by three men, in fact angels, who foretold that his wife Sarah, seen here listening in the doorway, would bear a child in spite of her age and the obvious disbelief of both (*Genesis* 18:1–15). This picture once hung in the guest rooms of the Escorial Palace, and the subject was chosen for its theme of offering hospitality to strangers. The three figures also symbolize the Trinity and have identical Christ-like faces.

In spite of being a deaf mute in poor health, Fernández de Navarrete trained in Venice, and was later known as 'the Spanish Titian', a nickname that the tenebrism, use of gesture and saturated colours here justify. He painted 32 pictures for chapels in the basilica of the Escorial, but the high altar was painted after his death.

2

3

4

2
Diego Velázquez de Silva
Seville 1599 – 1660 Madrid
Kitchen maid with the Supper at Emmaus,
*c.*1618
Canvas, 55 × 118 cm
Gift of Sir Alfred Beit Bt, 1987; NGI 4538
(Beit collection)

3
Juan Fernández 'El Labrador'
Active in Madrid 1630s
Still-life with citrons, a knife and pea-pods
on a stone ledge, 1630s
Canvas, 38 × 52 cm
Purchased, 1976; NGI 4186

4
Juan Carreño de Miranda
Gijon 1614 – 1685 Madrid
A Spanish noble child in its cradle, 1670s
Canvas, 94 × 114 cm
Purchased, 1959; NGI 1387

1

2

1–6

Bartolomé Esteban Murillo
Seville 1617 – 1682 Seville
The story of the Prodigal Son, 1660s
Each canvas, 104.5 × 134.5 cm
Gift of Sir Alfred Beit Bt, 1987; NGI
4540–4545 (Beit collection)
The story of the Prodigal Son (Luke
15:11–32), the younger of two brothers,
who takes his inheritance, spends it on
loose living, repents, then returns to be
forgiven by his father and brother, is here
depicted against the background of 17th-
century Seville. The series may have been
suggested by the similar life of Don Mi-
guel de Manara who commissioned a
major cycle of religious pictures from Murillo and Valdés Leal for the Hospital de la
Caridad. The variety of gesture, individual
characterization and passages of brilliant
colour mark out the series in Murillo's
work, but it is difficult to date them pre-
cisely. The first recorded owner was the
Marqués de Narros in the early 19th century. Several pictures were inspired by
Callot's etchings of the Prodigal Son, but
are here reinterpreted on a much larger
scale.

1 *The Prodigal Son receiving his portion*

2 *The departure of the Prodigal Son*

3 *The Prodigal Son feasting*

4 *The Prodigal Son driven out*

5 *The Prodigal Son feeding swine*

6 *The return of the Prodigal Son*

4

6

3

5

1   2

1
Francisco de Zurbarán
Fuente de Cantos 1598 – 1664 Madrid
The Immaculate Conception, 1660s
Canvas, 166 × 108.5 cm
Purchased, 1886; NGI 273

2
Francisco de Zurbarán
Fuente de Cantos 1598 – 1664 Madrid
St Rufina, early 1630s
Canvas, 176 × 107.5 cm
Purchased, 1933; NGI 962

3
Francisco de Goya
Fuendetodos 1746 – 1828 Bordeaux
El sueño (Sleep), c.1800
Canvas, 44.5 × 77 cm
Purchased, 1969 (Shaw fund); NGI 1928
This beautiful depiction of a sleeping
woman by Goya is both a rare subject for
him and a tender response to female
beauty. It is painted with the freedom of a
sketch: fluent strokes of near monochrome
paint are set off by highlights in yellow
and pink on the woman's brown hair, face
and white dress. Once thought to be an
overdoor for his friend Sebastian Martinez
in Cadiz, its style is now seen to place it
in the following decade, shortly before life
in Spain was disrupted by the French inva-
sion and when Goya was principally working as a court portraitist. It may have been
painted for Prime Minister Godoy, who
also commissioned the famous *Majas*.

3

4
Francisco de Goya
Fuendetodos 1746 – 1828 Bordeaux
'El Conde del Tajo', c.1800
Canvas, 62.5 × 52.5 cm
Purchased, 1908; NGI 600

4

67

1

1

Pablo Ruiz Picasso
Malaga 1881 – 1973 Mougins
Still life with a mandolin, 1924
Canvas, 101 × 158 cm
Máire MacNeill Sweeney bequest, 1987;
NGI 4522
On a bright tablecloth with lively arab-
esque border, Picasso arranged a pile of
textiles, a carafe or bottle and principally a
mandolin, described with Cubist simplic-
ity and painted like the rest in clear strong
colours. He painted several such works at
Juan-les-Pins on the Côte d'Azur during
the summer of 1924. Mediterranean trees
are indicated in silhouette through a
window. The unusually decorative design
and sensual delight in shapes recall Mat-
isse. Gone are the interlocked facets and
grey colours of earlier still life and col-
lage. Their presence is still felt in the haunting *Pierrot* by his close friend Juan Gris,
one of the last major works in a sequence
he painted of theatrical figures. Inspired
by his work for Diaghilev's *Ballets Russes*,
they follow the tradition of presenting the
masked clown as the artist's surrogate.

French School

Each Director of the Gallery has in his turn sought to improve and expand the range of French paintings so that today this school constitutes one of the most representative collections in the Gallery, strongest in seventeenth-, eighteenth- and nineteenth-century works.

When the Gallery opened to the public in 1864 only eight of the 125 paintings on view were French, with two of these on loan from the National Gallery, London. The three large altarpieces exhibited at the opening, *Christ curing one possessed* by Charles Antoine Coypel, *The Call of the Sons of Zebedee* by Bon Boulogne and Poerson's *Assumption of the Virgin* [p.71], were part of the 'job lot' bought in Rome in 1856. The large *Milo of Croton* presented by Arthur Guinness to the Gallery in the same year was at that time believed to be by David. It has subsequently been identified, by means of a sketch by Saint Aubin in the *Salon* catalogue of 1761, as the work exhibited by Jean-Jacques Bachelier in that year. Although a mere handful of French works were acquired in the remainder of the century, one of the most outstanding purchases of all was Poussin's moving mature work *The Lamentation over the body of Christ* [p.72], formerly in the collection of Sir William Hamilton.

A significant number of interesting seventeenth- and eighteenth-century works were acquired with the Milltown gift in 1902. The seventeen French paintings included in this gift served to strengthen what was still a rather fragmented French collection. A number have been reattributed over the years but fortunately such changes have tended to elevate rather than diminish their importance. The Gallery thus received its second Poussin, *The Holy Family*, Bertin's *The Finding of the cup in Benjamin's sack*, and Jean-François de Troy's *Bacchus and Ariadne*, as well as a number of important eighteenth-century works. Among these are two tiny, rare works by Jean-Etienne Lebel [p.76], three Paters, an important *bozzetto* of 1719 by François Lemoyne for a now destroyed altarpiece in St-Germain-des-Près in Paris, and two very fine *Lion hunts* by Joseph Parrocel.

The French school received a second vital boost following the tragic death of Sir Hugh Lane. As a result of his bequest, in 1918 the Gallery acquired a major work by Poussin, *Acis and Galatea* [p.72], of which the authorship, like the *Lamentation*, has never been doubted. Lane's bequest also included Poussin's *Bacchante and Satyr*, Lemaire's *Childhood of Bacchus* [p.73], the Claude *Juno confiding Io to the care of Argus* [p.73], two Chardins, the *Young governess* and the *Still life* [p.74], and Lancret's *La Malice* [p.77]. A number of French nineteenth-century pictures and drawings were bequeathed by

Edward Martyn in 1924. Martyn, like Lane, was one of the earliest Irish collectors of Impressionism and had bought most of these works in Paris – including Monet's *River scene, Autumn* [p.86] and two pastels by Degas, *Harlequins* and *Dancers in the dressing room* [p.88].

Thomas Bodkin, who became Director in 1927, must have realised that, despite its fine holding of seventeenth- and eighteenth-century paintings, the French school was still weak in the areas of portraiture and in nineteenth-century works; he immediately purchased portraits by Alexis-Simon Belle and Jean-Baptiste Perronneau [p.74]. George Furlong continued to build up the nineteenth-century collection, buying the Morisot [p.88] in 1936, the Blanche [p.90] in 1941 and Tissot's *View of Greenwich Pier* in 1943. He proposed a number of further purchases for the collection including a Gauguin and several paintings by Monet but all were rejected by the Board of Governors and Guardian. In 1950 Furlong resigned and Thomas McGreevy took over a few months later. At McGreevy's first board meeting he reported to the Board that Sir Alfred Chester Beatty had made a gift to the nation of some 90 paintings, mainly of the Barbizon school.

Fortunately, despite this enormous gift, McGreevy continued the slow, but steady pattern of purchasing started by Bodkin and Furlong. McGreevy added to the seventeenth century with the *Peasant family* by Jean Michelin, *The Adoration of the Shepherds* believed at that time to be by Louis Le Nain and now attributed to Mathieu Le Nain, and the fine portrait of Philippe Roettiers [p.75] painted by Largillière shortly after Roettiers was appointed Engraver General of the Mint of the King of Spain in the Low Countries in 1684. The small sketch of *A girl in a park* by Boucher, Nattier's portrait of Carlotta Frederika Sparre, Countess Fersen, and Courbet's portrait of Dr Adolphe Marlet [p.80] also number among McGreevy's purchases.

In the 1960s and 1970s a number of judicious additions were made by James White. Jacques Yverni's large picture combining the *Annunciation* and the *Immaculate Conception* is a rare panel dating from the early fifteenth century [p.70]. Gérard's portrait of Marie-Julie Bonaparte [p.79], painted 1808-09 for Napoleon to be hung in the Salon de Famille at St-Cloud, David's *Funeral of Patroclus* [p.78] and Fragonard's *Venus and Cupid* [p.76] are representative of three previously neglected aspects in the collection.

In the last decade five Impressionist and early twentieth-century paintings were acquired by Homan Potterton in a considered attempt to augment the holdings of this period in French painting [pp.86–89].

1

Jacques Yverni
Active Avignon 1410 – 1438
The Annunciation
Panel, 151 × 193 cm
Purchased, 1965 (Shaw fund); NGI 1780

2
Simon Vouet
Paris 1590 – 1649 Paris
The Four Seasons, c.1635
Canvas, diameter 113 cm
Purchased, 1970 (Shaw fund); NGI 1982

3

3
Charles Poerson
Lorraine 1609? – 1667 Paris
The Assumption of the Virgin, 1645/50
Canvas, 255 × 211 cm
Purchased, 1856; NGI 1896
This was one of the first French paintings
acquired by the Gallery and was formerly
in the collection of Cardinal Fesch in
Rome. A signed oil sketch for the painting
turned up recently and confirms the
attribution to Charles Poerson.

1

1
Nicolas Poussin
Les Andeleys 1594 – 1665 Rome
Acis and Galatea, c.1629/31
Canvas, 98 × 137 cm
Sir Hugh Lane bequest, 1918; NGI 814
Seated on a promontory overlooking the
sea, Polyphemus, the one-eyed giant, his
shepherd's crook laid aside, plays a love
song to Galatea on the syrinx (the pipes of
Pan). Galatea and her preferred lover, Acis,
sit in the foreground on a rocky outcrop,
shielded from his sight by the red drape
held up by the two *amorini* while tritons
and nereids play around them in the
waves. Mount Etna looms in the distance.

2

3

4

2
Nicolas Poussin
Les Andeleys 1594 – 1665 Rome
Lamentation over the body of Christ,
c.1655/60
Canvas, 94 × 130 cm
Purchased, 1882; NGI 214

3
Claude Lorrain
Chamagne 1600 – 1682 Rome
Juno confiding Io to the care of Argus, 1660
Canvas, 60 × 75 cm
Sir Hugh Lane bequest, 1918; NGI 763

4
Jean Lemaire
Dammartin 1598 – 1659 Gaillon
The childhood of Bacchus (or Romulus?)
Canvas, 163 × 140 cm
Sir Hugh Lane gift, 1918; NGI 800

1
Jean-Baptiste Perronneau
Paris 1715 – 1783 Amsterdam
Portrait of a man, 1766
Canvas, 72.5 × 58.5 cm
Purchased, 1929 (Lane fund); NGI 920

2
Jean-Baptiste Chardin
Paris 1699 – 1779 Paris
Still life, 1731
Canvas, 82.5 × 65 cm
Sir Hugh Lane bequest, 1918; NGI 799

1

2

74

3
Nicolas Largillière
Paris 1656 – 1746 Paris
Philippe Roettiers, c.1685
Canvas, 81 × 64 cm
Purchased, 1962; NGI 1729

4
Alexandre-François Desportes
Champigneulles 1661 – 1743 Paris
Group of dead game, 1707
Canvas, 91 × 73 cm
Sir Hugh Lane gift, 1914; NGI 671

3

4

1

2

1

Jean-Honoré Fragonard
Grasse 1732 – 1806 Paris
Venus and Cupid or *Day, c.*1766
Canvas, 114 × 133 cm
Purchased, 1978 (Shaw fund); NGI 4313
Untouched by the prevailing fashion for
neo-classicism in the second half of the
18th century, Fragonard made love one of
the principal themes in his paintings. Here
Venus, the goddess of love and fertility,
and her son Cupid are drawn in a gilded
chariot through the clouds by a pair of
doves. The painting was one of a series of
four overdoors representing the Hours of
the Day which were purchased by Hubert
Drouais for Madame du Barry to orna-
ment the former pavillion at Louve-
ciennes. Such decorative cycles were an
integral part of Rococo interiors; *Venus
and Cupid* is enlarged at the top and may
have been used again to decorate the new
pavillion which was begun in 1770.

2

Jean-Etienne Lebel
Active 1767 – 1774
Fête champêtre – dance
Canvas, 36 × 46 cm
Milltown gift, 1902; NGI 721
This tiny painting, along with its pendant,
Music, are among the few surviving recog-
nised works by this artist.

3

Nicolas Lancret
Paris 1690 – 1745 Paris
La Malice (Mischief)
Canvas, 36 × 29 cm
Sir Hugh Lane bequest, 1918; NGI 802

4

Jean-Baptiste Chardin
Paris 1699 – Paris 1779
Les Tours de cartes (Card-tricks), 1739?
Canvas, 31 × 39 cm
Purchased, 1898; NGI 478

3

4

1

1 and 2
Jacques-Louis David
Paris 1748 – 1825 Brussels
The Funeral of Patroclus, 1778
Canvas, 94 × 218 cm
Purchased, 1973 (Shaw fund); NGI 4060
David won the *Prix de Rome* in 1774 and
the following year went to study at the
French Academy in Rome. In 1776 the rule
was re-introduced whereby every year the
Director of the Academy should send back
a painting from each *pensionnaire* to the
Directeur général des Bâtiments in order to
judge each young artist's progress. This
picture, although signed and dated 1779,
was in fact painted in 1778 and sent to
Paris along with the works by the other
pensionnaires. David returned to Paris in
1780 and exhibited it at the *Salon* the following year, where it was highly praised.
Certainly, the antique subject matter
illustrating the virtue of self-sacrifice for
one's country was popular with Neoclassical artists. David himself was dissatisfied,
however, and went on to evolve a more
direct, concentrated style.

2

3

3
François Pascal Simon Gérard
Rome 1770 – Paris 1837
Marie-Julie Bonaparte, Queen of Spain, with
her two daughters Zenaïde and Charlotte,
1808-09
Canvas, 200 × 143.5 cm
Purchased, 1972 (Shaw fund); NGI 4055

1

2

1
Jean-Baptiste Corot and **Charles-François Daubigny**
Paris 1796 – 1875 Ville d'Avray;
Paris 1817 – 1878 Paris
Souvenir de Roquemaure-dans-le-Gard, 1853
Canvas, 142 × 205.5 cm
Purchased, 1931; NGI 950

2
Gustave Courbet
Ornans 1819 – 1877 La Tour de Peilz,
Vevey
Dr Adolphe Marlet, 1851
Canvas mounted on board, 56.5 × 46.5 cm
Purchased, 1962 (Shaw fund); NGI 1722

3
Eugène Delacroix
Charenton-St Maurice 1798 –
1863 Paris
Demosthenes on the seashore, 1859
Paper laid on panel, 47.5 × 58 cm
Purchased, 1934; NGI 964

4
Thomas Couture
Senlis 1815 – 1879 Villiers-le-Bel
La peinture réaliste (Realist painting), 1865
Panel, 56 × 45 cm
Sir Alfred Chester Beatty gift, 1950;
NGI 4220
Although Couture rebelled against the
academic system and the notion of 'serious painting' based on classical themes he
based his own methods of teaching on the
art of ancient Greece and the Renaissance
masters. He intended this picture as a satire on Realist painting. It has been interpreted as an attack on Gustave Courbet
but Couture is also harshly mocking the
unimaginative student who believes that
great art can be achieved purely through
observation. He is depicted slavishly copying the head of a dead pig, while using a
head of Jupiter for a seat when, Couture
implies, he would learn more by copying
that.

3

4

1

Eugène Fromentin
La Rochelle 1820 – 1876 St-Maurice
Falcon hunt, Algeria remembered, 1874
Canvas, 110.5 × 143.5
Sir Alfred Chester Beatty gift, 1950;
NGI 4231

2

Jean-Léon Gérôme
Vesoul 1824 – 1904 Paris
Guards at the door of a tomb
Canvas, 81.5 × 61.5 cm
Sir Alfred Chester Beatty gift, 1950;
NGI 4234

3

Ernest Meissonier
Lyons 1815 – 1891 Poissy
A group of cavalry in the snow, 1876
Panel, 37.5 × 47 cm
Sir Alfred Chester Beatty gift, 1950;
NGI 4263

4

James Tissot
Nantes 1836 – 1902 Buillon (Doubs)
Marguerite in church, c.1861
Canvas, 50.2 × 75.5 cm
Sir Alfred Chester Beatty gift, 1950;
NGI 4280

2

3

4

1

Léon Lhermitte
Mont-St-Père 1844 – 1925 Paris
Harvesters at Rest, 1888
Canvas, 96 × 75 cm
Sir Alfred Chester Beatty gift, 1950;
NGI 4255

2

Jules Breton
Courrières (Pas-de-Calais) 1827 –
1906 Paris
The gleaners, Courrières, 1854
Canvas, 93 × 138 cm
Sir Alfred Chester Beatty gift, 1950;
NGI 4213

Breton was greatly concerned with the
conditions of the lower social classes and,
as a consequence, with the political
changes which affected them. Themes
from peasant life constantly recur in his
work. *The gleaners* gave him the opportun-
ity to combine a scene set in his native
Courrières with a topical subject of the
day: a new law affecting the rights of
gleaners was passed in 1854. Breton's pictures were, nonetheless, immensely popular because he tempers his realism with a
touch of romanticism. He plays down the
misery and hardship of those forced by
circumstance to glean the remaining corn
after the harvest. His peasants are digni-
fied and the young girls beautiful. The
model for the young woman standing on
the right was Elodie, who later became
Breton's wife.

1

2

84

3

4

5

3
Eugène Boudin
Honfleur 1824 – 1898 Deauville
The Meuse at Dordrecht, 1882
Canvas, 117 × 159 cm
Sir Alfred Chester Beatty gift, 1950;
NGI 4212

4
Jean-François Millet
Cruchy 1814 – 1875 Barbizon
The stile
Canvas, 54 × 65 cm
Sir Alfred Chester Beatty gift, 1950;
NGI 4265

5
Jules-Jacques Veyrassat
Paris 1828 – 1893 Paris
Loading the corn
Canvas, 26.5 × 35 cm
Sir Alfred Chester Beatty gift, 1950;
NGI 4285

1

1
Claude Monet
Paris 1840 – 1926 Giverny
A river scene, autumn, c.1874
Canvas, 55 × 65 cm
Edward Martyn bequest, 1924; NGI 852

2
Camille Pissarro
Saint Thomas 1830 – 1903 Paris
Bouquet of flowers in a Chinese vase, c.1872
Canvas, 60 × 50.5 cm
Purchased, 1983 (Shaw fund); NGI 4459

3
Alfred Sisley
Paris 1839 – 1899 Moret-sur-Loing
Bords du Canal du Loing à St-Mammès,
1888
Canvas, 38 × 55 cm
Purchased, 1934 (Lane fund); NGI 966
This bright, sunlit picture of the Loing
canal is one of several Sisley painted at
St-Mammès in the 1880s. As he himself
explained his technique, 'You see I am in
favour of different techniques within the
same picture . . . The sunlight, in softening
the outlines of one part of the scene, will
clarify and illuminate another, and these
effects of light which seem real in a landscape ought to be interpreted in a material
way on the canvas.'

2

5th Jan '94

Dear Frank and Mary

Hope you don't already have this. Its a lovely representation of our pic. treasures. To get the parrots before C'mas + I waited for this

Love . Brenda.

3

4

4

Paul Signac
Paris 1863 – 1935 Paris
Lady on the terrace, 1898
Canvas, 73 × 92 cm
Purchased, 1982 (Shaw fund); NGI 4361
Signac was a follower of Georges Seurat
and the main theorist of the Neo-
Impressionist movement. After Seurat's
death Signac went to St-Tropez in 1892,
disillusioned with the art world in Paris.
St-Tropez was still unspoilt at that time
and indeed was only accessible by sea.
From that year and up until the first
World War Signac returned each year. In
Lady on the terrace, St-Tropez is the sleepy
town in the background of this still and
silent landscape.

1
Edgar Degas
Paris 1834 – 1917 Paris
Dancers in the dressing room, c.1880
Paper, 48.5 × 64 cm
Edward Martyn bequest, 1924; NGI 2740

2
Berthe Morisot
Bourges 1841 – 1895 Paris
Le Corsage noir, 1876
Canvas, 73 × 60 cm
Purchased, 1936; NGI 984

3
Kees van Dongen
Delfshaven 1877 – 1968 Monaco
Stella in a flowered hat, 1908
Canvas, 65 × 54 cm
Purchased, 1981 (Shaw fund); NGI 4355

4
Pierre Bonnard
Fontenay-aux-Roses 1867 –
1947 Le Cannet
Boy eating cherries, 1895
Board, 52 × 41 cm
Gift of Lord and Lady Moyne, 1982;
NGI 4356

3

4

89

1
Jacques Emile Blanche
Paris 1861 – 1941 Paris
James Joyce (1882-1941), 1934
Canvas, 82 × 65 cm
Purchased, 1941; NGI 1051

2
Chaim Soutine
Near Minsk 1893 – 1943 Paris
Man walking the stairs, 1922-23
Canvas, 81.5 × 65 cm
Purchased, 1984 (Shaw fund); NGI 4485

British School

The British school collection spans from the Tudor period to the present day, from Holbein the Younger (a copy) to Derek Hill. It has been slowly built up since the 1850s, with major additions from the Milltown gift and Sir Hugh Lane's bequest. The emphasis has tended to be on portraiture, particularly of Irish sitters, with the finest works from the Georgian era, also a celebrated collection of 35 Turner watercolours. The few sixteenth-century pictures are mainly versions of well-known portraits, excepting the *Second Earl of Essex* in decorative armour by William Segar and *Sir Walter Raleigh*, now attributed to Segar. Amongst seventeenth-century pictures are three works by Cornelius Johnson, Talbot family portraits by Wright [p.102], Wissing and Riley, a full-length of the cultivated *First Duke of Ormonde* by Lely (presented by the seventh Earl of Carlisle in 1864) and Kneller's *King William III returning from the Treaty of Rijswijk* (reduced from the subject in the Presence Chamber at Hampton Court).

The great treasures, though, are from the eighteenth century. William Hogarth's keen observation of character and manners is seen in an early satire, *A woman swearing a child to a grave citizen*, the 1740 portrait of dramatist Dr Benjamin Hoadly and particularly *The Western family* [p.93]. Here Thomas Western returns with dead game from hunting and joins his wife and mother at tea with the Reverend William Hatsell. On a larger scale, *The Mackinen children* [p.92] depicts Elizabeth and William with a French Rococo tenderness, as they are transfixed by the (symbolically transient) butterfly, sunflower and shells. Thomas Gainsborough's more sentimental view of childhood infuses *The cottage girl* [p.94], one of ten works by him in the Gallery, and similar in mood to his *Landscape with cattle*. His portraits range from an awkward study of a relative to suave images from his Bath period (*James Quin; General Johnston*) and the later *Duke of Northumberland*. Twelve paintings by his great contemporary Joshua Reynolds are equally diverse. The *Parody* [p.96] and three smaller caricature groups are juvenilia, the *Second Earl of Northington* and *First Marquess of Buckingham with his family* large

formal works. Most surprising is the sumptuously painted *Earl of Bellamont* [p.95], renowned for his vanity, who wears the robes and headpiece of the Order of the Bath as if appearing at a masquerade, accompanied by his namesake and emblem, the coote bird. The portrait of a lady by George Romney [p.98] typifies the strong colouring and neo-classical air of his best London portraits, before Italian travel led to the later style seen in *The artist's wife* and *Mary Tighe*. Other pictures of note include an Angelica Kauffmann painted in Ireland (*The Ely family*); Thomas Hudson's stately *Countess of Mountrath; Viscount Perceval* and *Falstaff's recruits* by Francis Hayman; the *Countess of Donegall* by Francis Cotes and *The Dublin Volunteers* [p.109] and *Marquess and Marchioness of Antrim* by Francis Wheatley, who was briefly in Dublin to escape creditors.

After Gainsborough the finest landscapes are two views of Tivoli by Richard Wilson [p.96], commissioned like Reynolds's *Parody* by Joseph Henry of Straffan. *Solitude* by Wilson is a more romantic work of 1762. The Regency period is again dominated by portraits. *Lady Elizabeth Foster* by Thomas Lawrence [p.97] appears in the guise of the Tiburtine Sibyl, with the Temple of the Sibyl at Tivoli in the stormy landscape beyond. *Sir John and Lady Clerk of Penicuik* [p.98] is a masterpiece by Raeburn, where the Scottish landscape is permeated by a soft, warm light found only in some of his most assured early portraits. It augments penetrating likenesses of the *Eleventh Earl of Buchan* and *Matthew Fortescue*. Artists abroad in the early nineteenth century such as Richard Bonington (*The Chibouk*) and the peripatetic George Chinnery (*W J. Binjian: Howqua*) contrast with John Constable (*Harnham Ridge*, an oil study) and David Wilkie (*The Marchioness of Lansdowne* and *Napoleon and Pope Pius VII at Fontainebleau*). The most significant Victorian painting is *Members of the Sheridan family* by Edwin Landseer, while among the few modern works are four Augustus John portraits, vigorous landscapes by Roger Fry and Matthew Smith (in the 1945 Miss Kennedy bequest), and an important portrait of James Joyce in Zurich, from the 1987 Máire MacNeill Sweeney bequest.

1

1
William Hogarth
London 1697 – 1764 London
The Mackinen children, 1747
Canvas, 180 × 143 cm
Sir Hugh Lane bequest, 1918; NGI 791

2
Philip Reinagle
Edinburgh? 1749 – 1833 London
Mrs Congreve with her children: Rebecca
Elmstone (died 1791), *with Ann* (1773-1814),
Thomas (1777-1832), *and Charlotte*
(1775-1845), 1782
Canvas, 80.5 × 106 cm
Edmund Russborough Turton gift, 1914;
NGI 676
In what may be the drawing room of
Eastcombe House, near Greenwich (now
demolished), Mrs Congreve awaits the re-
turn of Captain William Congreve
(1741-1814), whose prowess in manoeuv-
ring artillery is demonstrated by the pic-
ture seen behind her. This actual picture,

also by Reinagle, showing Captain
William's other son William (1772-1828) is
in the Gallery as well. In addition the Gallery holds the two Phillips paintings of
Captain Williams's parents which flank it
and Kneller's Kit-Cat portrait of his ances-
tor, the dramatist William Congreve,
shown over the mantelpiece (one of three
versions). Reinagle was working as a co-
pyist for Allan Ramsay at this date and
this sole conversation piece by him is frequently illustrated to show the layout and
contents of a 1780s interior. The chairs
and carver resemble Chippendale designs,
the back mirrors with girandoles an
example by Hepplewhite, while the floral
carpet is probably an Axminster.

2

3

3
William Hogarth
London 1697 – 1764 London
The Western family, 1730s
Canvas, 72 × 84 cm
Sir Hugh Lane bequest, 1918; NGI 792

Thomas Gainsborough
Sudbury 1727 – 1788 London
A view in Suffolk, c.1746
Canvas, 47 × 61 cm
Purchased, 1883; NGI 191

This crisply painted view of chalk pits by a
winding path combines motifs from
Gainsborough's native Suffolk with those
of Dutch pictures by Ruisdael and Wijnants, which he had studied. Even the
brooding clouds cannot detract from the
almost Rococo decorative quality and
treatment of paint. *Mrs Christopher Horton*
shows an equal sensitivity to painting
women, here the 'coquette beyond mea-
sure, artful as Cleopatra' as Horace Walpole described her, who married the Duke
of Cumberland without permission of his
brother King George III. *The cottage girl*, a
sad-faced girl in an evocative landscape
holding a broken pitcher, is a 'fancy picture' inspired by the sentimental genre
subjects of Murillo and has been ac-
claimed ever since it was painted. It
sold even then for more than a full-length
portrait.

1

2

Thomas Gainsborough
Sudbury 1727 – 1788 London
Mrs Christopher Horton (1743-1808), *later*
Duchess of Cumberland, 1766
Canvas, 75 × 62 cm
Sir Hugh Lane bequest, 1918; NGI 795

3

Thomas Gainsborough
Sudbury 1727 – 1788 London
The cottage girl, 1785
Canvas, 174 × 124.5 cm
Gift of Sir Alfred Beit Bt, 1987; NGI 4529
(Beit collection)

3

94

Joshua Reynolds
Plympton 1723 – 1792 London
Charles Coote, first Earl of Bellamont
(1738-1800), in robes of the Order of the
Bath, c.1774

Canvas, 245 × 162 cm
Purchased, 1875; NGI 216

1

2

1
Joshua Reynolds
Plympton 1723 – 1792 London
Parody of Raphael's *'School of Athens'*,
1751
Canvas, 97 × 135 cm
Milltown gift, 1902; NGI 734
Raphael's stately fresco of the triumph of
philosophy, in the Vatican Stanza della
Segnatura, is here transformed into carica-
tures of Irish and British tourists visiting
Rome. Each physical trait or personal
vanity has been brilliantly exaggerated
with a Gothic setting replacing a classical
one. Reynolds ironically later commented
that satire 'must corrupt the taste of a portrait painter only interested in the perfec-
tions of the sitter'. At the centre, the
portly Joseph Leeson, later first Earl of
Milltown, replaces Plato. His nephew,
Joseph Henry, lounges on the steps where
the Cynic Diogenes should be. He commissioned the parody, which cost him 80
scudi. To his left in place of Pythagoras
and his students are the painter Thomas
Patch and a trio of James Caulfeild, later
first Earl of Charlemont (recorder), Sir
Thomas Kennedy (flute) and Mr Phelps
('cello).

2
Richard Wilson
Penegoes 1713? – 1782 near Mold
*The Palace of Maecenas, Tivoli, and distant
view of Rome*, 1752
Canvas, 50 × 66 cm
Milltown gift, 1902; NGI 746

3

3
Thomas Lawrence
Bristol 1769 – 1830 London
Lady Elizabeth Foster (1759-1824), *later
Duchess of Devonshire*, 1805
Canvas, 240 × 148 cm
Sir Hugh Lane bequest, 1918; NGI 788

1

2

3

Irish School

The virtual absence of easel painting in Ireland until the second half of the seventeenth century is usually attributed to the previous political instability of the country; another factor is undoubtedly the lack of interest in the visual arts by the vast majority of the soldier-planters in those earlier centuries.

John Michael Wright (1617-94) worked in England, Scotland and Ireland, executing portraits of remarkable quality; he excelled in treating fine clothes, the richer the better, armour and garlands or bunches of flowers: a good example is his double portrait of the young Talbot sisters, Ladies Catherine and Charlotte [p.102]. Wright also relished stylish backgrounds.

Garrett Morphey (active 1680-1716) is a painter whose clientele appears to have been almost exclusively Jacobite. The Gallery has a few good portraits by him; particularly characteristic are works in which the sitter is placed in a landscape, lying on the ground with head supported by one arm. This pose from the time of Hilliard and Oliver is taken to indicate mourning or melancholia.

Melancholia is well represented in the Gallery by Jervas's *Jane Seymour Conway*. Despite initial training, some ten years in Rome, and further studies in London, Charles Jervas (c.1675-1739) is extremely uneven as a painter; however, his portraits of Dean Swift in the National Portrait Gallery, London, and *Lady Mary Wortley Montagu* [p.104] are noteworthy. He was appointed Principal Painter to the King following the death of Kneller in 1723.

James Latham (1696-1747) studied in Antwerp, and was actually admitted to the painter's guild there. He appears to have settled in Ireland, and had a lively practice in portraiture, moving in Jacobite and Williamite circles alike. The high standard of his best works, such as *Bishop Clayton and his wife* [p.103], caused many of his portraits to be attributed to Hogarth. The first half of the eighteenth century produced a fine crop of portraitists, among whom one may mention Anthony Lee, John Lewis and Philip Hussey (1713-83) [p.103].

Another portraitist of high quality is Thomas Frye (1710-62), whose career was entirely in England. The elegance of some of his portraits must surely be attributed to the influence of Philip Mercier, and perhaps to Amigoni's English paintings. Frye was a founder of the famous Bow porcelain factory, and also its first manager; this undertaking did not deflect him from portraiture. Shortly before his death he completed some of the finest mezzotints of the century. Frye was a very important influence on Joseph Wright of Derby.

Nathaniel Hone the Elder (1718-84) is another example of an Irish portraitist who developed a flourishing practice in London, and he was to become a foundation member of the Royal Academy in 1768. At the Academy's first exhibition in the following year one of Hone's exhibits was *The piping boy* [p.105]. Hone's finest works were self-portraits and portraits of children.

A second Irishman, George Barret (1728-84), was also a foundation member of the Royal Academy. He trained in Dublin under the tutelage of James Mannin ('The Frenchman'), not one of whose drawings or paintings is known today. When one considers Barret's series of landscapes for the future Lord Milltown's country mansion, Russborough, or a superlative large *Landscape*, signed and dated in the 1750s, one can only conclude that aspiring artists were shown engravings of works by such artists as Vernet, van Lint, Panini and Zuccarelli. On the other hand, they went out into the countryside, Barret on Edmund Burke's advice, and returned with sufficient sketches to enable them to paint a masterpiece like the Gallery's *Powerscourt Waterfall* by Barret [p.111]. Not satisfied with local patronage, Barret went to England, and became a resounding success, earning more than £2,000 a year, and spending even more! Barret travelled up and down Great Britain, and there are series of landscapes painted in and around the estates of Inveraray Castle, Dalkeith Park, Welbeck and Windsor.

Among other notable Irish landscape painters were George Mullins, James Coy, Richard and Robert Carver, and Thomas Roberts (1748-78). The last named is well represented in the Gallery by a set of four canvases showing the old Lucan House and its demesne [p.110]. Roberts also made a magnificent set of views of Carton demesne (now dispersed); to these were added paintings by William Ashford (c.1746-1824) who was commissioned by the Duke of Leinster after Roberts's early death. An *Idyllic landscape* from Carton by Ashford is in the Gallery, as is a splendid panoramic view of Dublin, taken from Chapelizod, a village to the west of the city [p.111]. Ashford lived to become first President of the Royal Hibernian Academy in 1823, but died before the first exhibition in 1826.

Hugh Douglas Hamilton (c.1739-1808) was successful in Dublin, London, Rome and Dublin again. In Rome he painted some of his finest works, such as the *Frederick Hervey, Bishop of Derry and Earl of Bristol, with his granddaughter Lady Caroline Crichton* [p.106]. Hamilton also painted some mythological canvases, especially after his return to Dublin in the 1790s, probably to relieve the boredom of formal portraiture.

James Barry (1741-1806), born in Cork, and largely self-taught, went to Rome again with the advice and support of Edmund Burke. Having returned to London, he became a member of the Royal Academy, in 1773, and shortly afterwards Professor of Painting. In the Great Room of the Society of Arts at the Adelphi in London he executed a heroic series of paintings depicting *The Progress of Human Culture*. This achievement together with canvases such as *The death of Adonis* [p.107] ensure Barry a prominent place in history painting in these islands. Also here are his *Adam and Eve*, painted in Rome, and a powerful self-portrait as Timanthes [p.107]. Barry had the dubious distinction of being the only member of the Royal Academy to be expelled.

The Romantic movement affected Ireland, and a major exponent was James Arthur O'Connor (1792-1841), whose 'black on black with froth' canvases painted in the Dargle valley of Co. Wicklow are quite awesome. O'Connor's friend Francis Danby, who remained in England after their initial visit there, following success with view paintings, burst into the Romantic movement with sometimes apocalyptical ferocity. His *The Opening of the Sixth Seal* [p.112] is a splendid example of his dramatic work.

The Pre-Raphaelite movement made little impact on indigenous Irish art. But the elusive Matthew William Lawless (1837-64), with a painting like *The sick call* [p.114], belongs generically to that movement; so, too, do some of the highly finished watercolours of Frederic William Burton (1816-1900) [p.116].

Nineteenth-century history painting's greatest exponent was Daniel Maclise (1806-70). The wallsize *Marriage of Strongbow and Aoife* [p.113] demonstrates to visitors to the Gallery a sample of his enormous undertakings for the Houses of Parliament at Westminster.

Leading the way to France for *plein-air* painting was Nathaniel Hone the younger, who arrived at Barbizon about 1855. Among his many friends were Corot and Harpignies, and he readily adopted the lessons of his colleagues. Of independent means, Hone saw no need to chase every stylistic development, and when he eventually settled back in north Co.Dublin he had no reason to alter his style radically. Hone has been rather underestimated but he was the harbinger of what Irish painters of a slightly later date achieved in Barbizon, Fontainebleau and Brittany.

Following Hone to France were, among others, O'Conor, Lavery, Osborne and Thaddeus. Roderic O'Conor (1860-1940) had a personal income, but this did not deter him from working hard. He has a rare distinction; he painted in the Fauve manner in the very conceptual years of that movement. The apparently exotic *Farm at Lezaven* anticipates the real rugged Fauve idiom of *A landscape with rocks* [both p.120].

Sir John Lavery earned success after hard early years. At Grez-sur-Loing he painted some exquisitely idyllic riverside scenes, and he was always happy painting by the water whether at Tangiers or along the Thames. He was extremely successful as a portrait painter, and served as an Official War Artist. Lavery had a beautiful wife, Hazel, as can be seen in *The artist's studio* [p.123], just one of several enormous canvases successfully resolved.

Walter Osborne (1859-1903) arrived in France via the Academy of Antwerp, absorbed the lessons of his fellow painters, but really only reached a freedom and lightness of brush when family circumstances compelled him to return to Dublin. Henry Thaddeus (1859-1929) was well trained by the time he arrived in Brittany, where he executed some of his finest works, including *Market day, Finistère* [p.119].

Richard Thomas Moynan (1856-1906) remained a more realist painter than many of his Irish contemporaries. There is vigour in the skilfully composed '*Military manoeuvres*', one of the most popular paintings in the Irish Rooms, with children and adults alike.

Leech, Henry, Kavanagh, Purser, and countless more Irish painters matured after sojourns in Flanders or France, or both. One of the greatest Irish artists at the beginning of the twentieth century was Sir William Orpen (1878-1931), who, while making a fortune as a society portrait painter in London, came back each year to teach a course at the Metropolitan School of Art in Dublin (and to imbibe in Davy Byrne's and eat at Jammet's). This devotion laid the foundation for Irish painting for at least the ensuing 50 years. Like Lavery, he was called to serve as an Official War Artist, a task executed with consummate skill. World War I took its toll on Orpen, however; the horrors of the trenches and man's inhumanity affected the painter for the rest of his life. His spirits were lifted from time to time when he painted a mistress like Yvonne Aubicq, either naked or dressed.

In a superb composition like Orpen's *The Holy Well* [p.125], the artist's attitude to Ireland's past has a satirical edge. By contrast the great individualist Jack B Yeats (1871-1957) from his earliest graphic work reveals a total absorption in the people, places and legends encountered in his youth in the Sligo area. As he developed, the precise nature of the sources became diffused in an evolving technique. In the works of his maturity the spectator is invited into a world of mystery built on solid, but now invisible, foundations. The title bestowed on a late Yeats is really only an invitation to dream. Yeats is not the product of any school or master; he is his Irish self, and yet a clarion to the world.

1

1
John Michael Wright
London 1617 – 1694 London
The Ladies Catherine (born *c*.1671) *and*
Charlotte Talbot (born *c*.1676), 1679
Canvas, 131.1 × 110.5 cm
Purchased, 1976; NGI 4184

2

3

2

Philip Hussey
Cloyne, Co.Cork 1713 – 1783 Dublin
Interior with members of a family, 1750s
Canvas, 62 × 76 cm
Purchased, 1978 (Shaw fund); NGI 4304

3

James Latham
Co.Tipperary 1696 – 1747 Dublin
Bishop Robert Clayton (1695-1758) and his
wife Katherine (died 1766), 1730s
Canvas, 128 × 175 cm
Purchased, 1982; NGI 4370

1

1

Charles Jervas
Shinrone, Co.Offaly c.1675 –
1739 London
Lady Mary Wortley Montagu (1689-1762)
standing by a clavicytherium, 1720s
Canvas, 214.5 × 126 cm
Louis Cohen gift, 1981; NGI 4342

Lady Mary Wortley Montagu typifies the
free-thinking woman of the 18th century.
Daughter of the future Duke of Kingston,
she was an intellectual, beauty and wit,
whose circle included Pope, Addison and
Walpole. Her husband's appointment as
ambassador to Constantinople in 1716-18
made her an enthusiast for everything
Turkish, from dress to childhood inocula-
tion against smallpox. In 1739 she left
England with an Italian lover and her fascinating letters were only fully published
in 1836. Jervas painted her at least six
times, mostly in Turkish-style clothes, as
here, and in a pendant portrait in the Gallery. She poses by a type of upright harpsi-
chord, copied from Sacchi's *Marc'Antonio
Pasqualini* (Metropolitan Museum, New
York). Kneller's influence is evident in the
stylized figure; Lady Mary thought Jervas
would improve his art by studying naked
women in the Turkish baths.

2

Nathaniel Hone the Elder
Dublin 1718 – 1784 London
The conjurer, 1775
Canvas, 145 × 173 cm
Purchased, 1966 (Shaw fund); NGI 1790

Hone the Elder caused an uproar when he
submitted *The conjurer* for exhibition in
the Royal Academy, London. It was re-
fused ostensibly because there was a nude
caricature of artist Angelica Kauffmann;
this was painted over with artists at a
table, but can still be seen in a sketch in
the Tate Gallery, London. In fact the true
offence was the attack on her friend Sir
Joshua Reynolds, the President of the
Royal Academy, for plagiarism in bor-
rowing poses from Old Master paintings to
ennoble his portraits. The conjurer, one of
Reynolds's own models, holds a print of
Raphael's *Diadem Madonna*, where truth is
revealed to man, and gestures in the pose
of the *Apollo Belvedere* to create a picture
in a magic fire from a cascade of Old
Master prints. Hone the Elder preferred
Dutch realism to Italian artifice and even
The piping boy, inspired by Venetian pas-
torals, is also a portrait of his son.

3

Nathaniel Hone the Elder
Dublin 1718 – 1784 London
The piping boy (John Camillus, 1759-1836,
son of the artist), 1769
Canvas, 36 × 31 cm
Purchased, 1896; NGI 440

2

3

2

1
Hugh Douglas Hamilton
Dublin c.1739 – 1808 Dublin
Frederick Hervey, Bishop of Derry and
fourth Earl of Bristol (1730-1803), with his
granddaughter Lady Caroline Crichton
(1779-1856), in the gardens of the Villa
Borghese, Rome, c.1788
Canvas, 230 × 199 cm
Purchased, 1981 (Lane fund); NGI 4350
The Earl-Bishop was an inveterate travel-
ler, collector and builder. While tending to
pastoral duties, he frequently visited
Rome and also commissioned two Irish
country mansions and a third house at
Ickworth in Suffolk. His granddaughter accompanied her mother to Rome in 1787
and has here put down her drawing folio
to point out a relief of the Seasons on a
Roman altar of the twelve gods. The Earl-
Bishop may have wished to purchase this
unusual antique, then in the Borghese collection, but was outbid by Napoleon I (it is
now in the Louvre). The tree-lined lake behind the altar is also real and was laid out
by Scottish artist Jacob More, with a
Temple of Aesculapius designed by Marco
Asprucci. Hamilton was in Rome 1778-91,
developing his full potential in the circle
of the Neoclassical sculptor Canova, who
was a close friend. This picture is probably
Hamilton's masterpiece.

2
James Barry
Cork 1741 – 1806 London
The Death of Adonis, 1775
Canvas, 100 × 126 cm
Gift of Mr and Mrs R Field, 1959; NGI 1393

3
James Barry
Cork 1741 – 1806 London
Self-portrait as Timanthes, c.1780,
completed 1803
Canvas, 76 × 63 cm
Purchased, 1934; NGI 971

3

1

1
Thomas Hickey
Dublin 1741 – 1824 Madras
An actor between the Muses of Tragedy and
Comedy, 1781
Canvas, 102 × 128 cm
Purchased, 1925; NGI 862

2
Thomas Hickey
Dublin 1741 – 1824 Madras
An Indian lady, possibly Jemdanee, bibi of
William Hickey, 1787
Canvas, 102 × 127 cm
Sir Alec Martin gift, 1959; NGI 1390

3
Nathaniel Grogan
Cork *c*.1740 – 1807 Cork
Tivoli, near Cork, 1780s?
Canvas, 93 × 166 cm
Purchased, 1973 (Shaw fund); NGI 4074

4
Francis Wheatley
London 1747 – 1801 London
The Dublin Volunteers on College Green,
4th November 1779, 1779-80
Canvas, 175 × 323 cm
Gift of the fifth Duke of Leinster, 1891;
NGI 125

2

3

4

1

2

3

1
Thomas Roberts
Waterford 1748 – 1778 Lisbon
Ideal landscape, c.1770
Canvas, 112 × 153 cm
Purchased, 1972; NGI 4052

2
Thomas Roberts
Waterford 1748 – 1778 Lisbon
Lucan House and demesne, Co. Dublin,
c.1770
Canvas, 60.5 × 100 cm
Purchased, 1983 (Shaw fund); NGI 4463

3
Thomas Roberts
Waterford 1748 – 1778 Lisbon
Landscape with a river and horses
Canvas, 42.5 × 52.5 cm
Purchased, 1877; NGI 116

4

5

4
George Barret
Dublin 1728/32 – 1784 London
Powerscourt Waterfall, Co.Wicklow, c.1760
Canvas, 100 × 127 cm
Purchased, 1880; NGI 174

5
William Ashford
Birmingham *c.*1746 – 1824 Dublin
Panorama of Dublin from Chapelizod,
1794/8
Canvas, 114 × 183 cm
Purchased, 1976; NGI 4138

1

1

Francis Danby
Near Wexford 1793 – 1861 Exmouth
The Opening of the Sixth Seal (Revelations, 6:12), 1828
Canvas, 185 × 255 cm
Purchased, 1871; NGI 162

The haunting visions of St John on the island of Patmos, recorded in *Revelations*, foretell the Day of Judgement, after the destruction predicted in the Old Testament. As the Sixth Seal is broken, the earth erupts like a volcano and humans cower against a blood red moon and the jagged lightning that herald divine judgement. Constable wrote that 'the subject is from Revelations but might pass for the burning of Sodom' and it was such pictures of biblical and natural disasters, bordering on melodrama, that brought Danby more success in the 1820s than the pastoral landscapes he had been painting in Bristol. A mezzotint of it was published by Colnaghi in 1830, by which time William Beckford had purchased it for his eccentric house at Fonthill. Even in 1843, it still drew crowds and acclaim when exhibited in New York.

3

4

2
James Arthur O'Connor
Dublin 1792 – 1841 London
A thunderstorm: the frightened wagoner,
1832
Canvas, 65 × 76 cm
Brian McCormick gift, 1972; NGI 4041

3
Daniel Maclise
Cork 1806 – 1870 London
The Marriage of Strongbow and Aoife (the
Earl of Pembroke and Princess Aoife), 1854
Canvas, 309 × 505 cm
Sir Richard Wallace gift, 1879; NGI 205

4
James Arthur O'Connor
Dublin 1792 – 1841 London
The mill, Ballinrobe, Co.Mayo, c.1818
Canvas, 42 × 71 cm
Purchased, 1970; NGI 4011

1
Edwin Hayes
Bristol 1819 – 1904 London
An emigrant ship, Dublin Bay, sunset, 1853
Canvas, 58 × 86 cm
Miss Mary S Kilgour gift, 1951; NGI 1209

2
Michael George Brennan
Castlebar, Co.Mayo 1839 –
1871 Algiers
A vine pergola on Capri, 1866
Canvas, 56 × 75 cm
Purchased, 1873; NGI 153

3
Matthew James Lawless
Dublin 1837 – 1864 London
The sick call, 1863
Canvas, 63 × 103 cm
Purchased, 1925; NGI 864

4
William Mulready
Ennis, Co.Clare 1786 – 1863 London
The toy-seller, 1857-63
Canvas, 112 × 142 cm
Purchased, 1891; NGI 387

5
Richard Rothwell
Athlone, Co.Westmeath 1800 –
1868 Rome
The mother's pastime, 1844
Canvas, 93 × 79 cm
Purchased, 1942; NGI 1102

1

2

3

4

5

1

Augustus Nicholas Burke
Dublin c.1849 – 1891 Florence
A Connemara girl, 1880s?
Canvas, 63 × 48 cm
Mrs Ida Monahan gift, 1951; NGI 1212
This idyllic vision of a beautiful girl with perfect features gathering heather in the west of Ireland while her goats graze is a rare image of rural life in the 19th century – however artificial it may now seem, ignoring the horrors of famine and political turmoil. It recalls both the ideal rural world of Breton and the *plein-air* approach of Bastien-Lepage, with a sentimental peasant child in high detail against a more generalised setting. Burke visited Pont-Aven in 1876, and did travel to Connemara, where artists rarely went in his time, though Burton had been there in the 1840s and Henry would go in 1910. His early Brittany pictures are sketch-like and generally sunlit, while his later work is more sombre. He exhibited Connemara scenes in Dublin from the early 1880s.

2

Frederic William Burton
Corofin, Co.Clare 1816 – 1900 London
The meeting on the turret stairs, 1864
Watercolour on paper, 95.5 × 60.8 cm
Miss Margaret Stokes bequest, 1900; NGI 2358

3

John Butler Yeats
Tullylish, Co.Down 1839 –
1922 New York
William Butler Yeats (1865-1939), *poet, dramatist and son of the artist*, 1900
Canvas, 77 × 64 cm
Cornelius Sullivan gift, 1926; NGI 872

4
Sarah Purser
Dublin 1848 – 1943 Dublin
Le petit déjeuner (Maria Feller, singer, at
breakfast), 1885
Canvas, 35 × 27 cm
Richard Irvine Best bequest, 1959; NGI
1424

5
Richard Thomas Moynan
Dublin 1856 – 1906 Dublin
'Military manoeuvres', 1891
Canvas, 148 × 240 cm
Purchased, 1982; NGI 4364

3

4

5

1

2

3

1
Walter Frederick Osborne
Dublin 1859 – 1903 Dublin
Near St Patrick's Close, an old Dublin street,
1887
Canvas, 69 × 51 cm
Purchased, 1921; NGI 836

2
Walter Frederick Osborne
Dublin 1859 – 1903 Dublin
Apple gathering, Quimperlé, 1883
Canvas, 58 × 46 cm
Patrick Sherlock bequest, 1940; NGI 1052

3
Walter Frederick Osborne
Dublin 1859 – 1903 Dublin
*In a Dublin park, light and shade, c.*1895
Canvas, 71 × 91 cm
Purchased, 1944; NGI 1121

4
Henry Jones Thaddeus
Cork 1859 – 1929 London?
Market day, Finistère, 1882
Canvas, 201 × 132 cm
Purchased, 1986; NGI 4513
Two of the finest Irish *plein-air* scenes
were painted within a year of each other.
Thaddeus had been at the Académie Julian
in Paris in 1880-81 before coming to Brittany, while Osborne was at the Antwerp
Academy 1881-83. *Market day* shows the
beach at Concarneau, where a young
woman in characteristic Plougastel costume pauses to inspect the local shellfish
and chestnuts. Her prominence is due to
the sharply painted detail of her costume
in an overall blue-grey tonality, and she
was no doubt painted in the disused
chapel where Thaddeus had his studio.
Apple gathering by Osborne is smaller and
more tightly painted, but is equally
memorable, as Osborne's favourite subjects, children, work in an orchard against
the tower of St Michel. The sombre
colouring is relieved by a range of subtle
greens. Later, Osborne's pictures became
closer to Renoir as he explored effects of
sunlight and used his brush more freely.

4

1

2

1
Roderic O'Conor
Milton, Co.Roscommon 1860 –
1940 Neuil-sur-Layon
Farm at Lezaven, Finistère, 1894
Canvas, 72 × 93 cm
Purchased, 1961; NGI 1642
After studying with Moynan at the
Antwerp Academy 1883-84, O'Conor discovered the Intimiste painters and Van
Gogh's work in Paris before spending over
a decade at Pont-Aven from 1890 to 1904,
where the stimulus of Gauguin inspired
some of his finest pictures. This farm was
a favourite studio for avantgarde artists on
the outskirts of Pont-Aven. The striped
divisionist brushwork in pink, maroon and
green fuses everything into a single band
of bright colour. The dilute paint gives a
more lyrical feel than the heavier use of
paint in some of O'Conor's peasant
studies. Having returned to Paris, O'Conor
exhibited with the Fauves and his work
changed accordingly.

2
Roderic O'Conor
Milton, Co.Roscommon 1860 –
1940 Neuil-sur-Layon
Landscape with rocks, c.1913
Canvas, 38 × 46 cm
Purchased, 1973; NGI 4057

3
William John Leech
Dublin 1881 – 1968 Guildford
Quimperlé – the goose girl, c.1910
Canvas, 72 × 91 cm
Purchased, 1970; NGI 4009

4
William John Leech
Dublin 1881 – 1968 Guildford
Convent garden, Brittany, c.1912
Canvas, 132 × 106 cm
Mrs May Bottrell gift, 1952; NGI 1245

3

4

1

2

3

1
Nathaniel Hone the Younger
Dublin 1831 – 1917 Raheny,
Co.Dublin
Pastures at Malahide, c.1905
Canvas, 82 × 124 cm
Nathaniel Hone the Younger gift, 1907;
NGI 588

2
Paul Henry
Belfast 1876 – 1958 Enniskerry,
Co.Wicklow
Launching the currach, 1910/11
Canvas, 41 × 60 cm
Purchased, 1968; NGI 1869

3
Paul Henry
Belfast 1876 – 1958 Enniskerry,
Co.Wicklow
The potato diggers, 1912
Canvas, 51 × 46 cm
Purchased, 1968; NGI 1870

4

4
John Lavery
Belfast 1856 – 1941 Rossenarra,
Co.Kilkenny
The artist's studio: Lady Hazel Lavery
(c.1887-1955), with her daughter Alice and
step-daughter Eileen, 1910-13
Canvas, 344 × 274 cm
Purchased, 1959; NGI 1644
In witty homage to *Las Meninas* by
Velázquez, Lavery and his wife are seen
reflected in a mirror as he paints his family in his London studio at Cromwell
Place. He met Hazel Martyn, daughter of a
Chicago industrialist, when she was painting at Brittany in 1904. She was both
beautiful and a leader of fashion, and her
political services to Ireland were rewarded
by being asked to sit as a model for
Lavery's Cathleen ni Houlihan, who ap-
peared on the first Irish banknotes and
survives in the present watermark on
them. Lavery originally painted himself,
like Velázquez, standing with an easel near
the viewer, but is now seen only in the
reflected mirror. The Moorish servant,
entering with a salver of fruit, was called
Aida. The large dog was Rodney Stone.
Over the mantelpiece can just be seen
Idonia in Morocco (Glasgow Art Gallery),
while a portrait of Queen Mary (Royal
Collection) is on an easel.

1
William Orpen
Stillorgan, Co.Dublin 1878 –
1931 London
The Vere Foster family, 1907
Canvas, 198 × 198 cm
Purchased, 1951; NGI 1199

2
Seán Keating
Limerick 1889 – 1977 Dublin
An Allegory, 1925
Canvas, 102 × 130 cm
Gift of the Friends of the National
Collections of Ireland, 1952; NGI 1236

3
William Orpen
Stillorgan, Co.Dublin 1878 –
1931 London
The holy well, 1916
Tempera on canvas, 234 × 186 cm
Purchased, 1971; NGI 4030
From 1913 to 1916 Orpen painted several
pictures which relate to the Celtic Revival,
but are frequently satirical. *The holy well*
mocks the superstition of Irish peasants
who come to drink and wash in a sup-
posedly miraculous holy well. The start-
ling quality of the picture comes from its
size, the newly invented artificial tempera
paint and the juxtaposition of naked and
clothed figures, particularly the one with a
beret, a portrait of Orpen's pupil Seán
Keating. Keating brought costumes from
the Aran islands to Orpen in London, presumably also photographs of the medieval
beehive huts, ruined church and Celtic
Cross which he includes. Keating recorded
that the fine preliminary drawings recalled
Ingres. There are also echoes of the Old
Masters in various figures and gestures.

1

2

3

1

1
Jack B Yeats
London 1871 – 1957 Dublin
The Liffey swim, 1923
Canvas, 61 × 91 cm
Gift of the trustees of the Haverty bequest,
1931; NGI 941

2
Jack B Yeats
London 1871 – 1957 Dublin
For the Road, 1951
Canvas, 61 × 92 cm
Gift of Mr and Mrs Frank Vickerman, 1978;
NGI 4309

3
Jack B Yeats
London 1871 – 1957 Dublin
Grief, 1951
Canvas, 102 × 153 cm
Purchased, 1965 (Shaw fund); NGI 1769

2

3

Index